FULL STEAM AHEAD

A Step-by-Step Guide to Project Management
From Start to Finish

By Dr. Brian Haywood, DBA, PMP

ISBN (Paperback): 978-1-968440-11-4
ISBN (Digital / eBook): 978-1-968440-12-1
ISBN (Hardback): 978-1-968440-10-7

Enhanced Learning Edition: 978-1-968440-13-8

Published by Scale Matrix LLC
An imprint of Knight Publishing
www.FullSteamAheadPM.com

Cover and interior design by Scale Matrix, LLC
This is a work of original nonfiction.

Printed in the United States of America
First Edition

Table of Contents

Dedication 14

Author Biography.. 15

Introduction - Welcome Aboard 18

What You Will Learn.. 22

Project Framework 24

Project 1 - The Project Management Plan 25

Choosing Your Project.. 26

Building Your Project Management Plan....................... 27

Business Case 27

Figure 1.1 Example Business Case............................. 28

Project Charter... 28

Figure 1.2 Example Project Charter 30

Stakeholder Register.. 31

Stakeholder Matrix 32

Figure 1.3 Stakeholder Matrix.................................. 32

Requirements Document 32

Project Scope Statement (Scope Baseline).................... 33

Activity List... 34

Figure 1.4 Example Activity List 35

Network Diagram 35

Critical Path 36

Figure 1.5 Example Network Diagram........................ 37

Figure 1.6 Example Critical Path 38

Activity Cost Estimates 39

Activity Cost with ROM (Cost Baseline)..................... 39

Figure 1.7 Example Activity Cost with ROM 41

Quality Metrics 42

Team Roles and Responsibilities 43

Preferred Communication Methods.................................. 43

Figure 1.8 Preferred Communication Plan 44

Risk Register.. 44

Figure 1.9 Example Risk Register 45

Risk Responses 45

Procurement Planning.. 46

Final Deliverable 47

Chapter 1 – Welcome Aboard 54

⚓ A Journey Begins... 56

What Is a Project? 58

Projects vs. Operations.. 59

The Five Process Groups.. 60

Project Constraints 60

Figure 1.1.1 Triple Constraints 62

The Role of the Project Manager 63

Why Project Management Matters.. 63

Choosing Your Project.. 65

Full Steam Ahead - Process Port 67

📓 Captain's Log: Discussion Board 69

Chapter 2: Scope Shores 70

⚓ Entering Scope Shores.. 72

Why Scope Matters 72

What Is Project Scope? 73

The Two Types of Scope (Critical Concept) 74

Scope Creep (The Hidden Danger) 75

The Work Breakdown Structure (WBS)............................ 76

Figure 2.1 Example Work Breakdown Structure........... 77

Real-World Example: Building a house 77

Connecting to Your Project (Project 1) 80

Full Steam Ahead - Process Port 81

End-of-Chapter Questions... 82

Captain's Log: Discussion Board 83

Chapter 3 – Schedule Shoals 84

Entering Schedule Shoals 86

What Is Project Scheduling? 86

Why Scheduling Matters.. 88

Understanding Task Dependencies.................................. 89

From WBS to Schedule.. 91

Critical Path (The River's Main Channel) 92

Real-World Example: Building a House - Project Timeline
.... 94

Common Scheduling Mistakes... 97

Connecting to Your Project (Project 1) 97

Full Steam Ahead - Process Port 100

End-of-Chapter Questions... 101

Captain's Log: Discussion Board 102

Chapter 4 – Cost & Quality Coves 103

Entering Cost & Quality Coves 105

Understanding Project Cost.. 106

Cost Estimation 108

The Project Budget (Cost Baseline) 110

Cost and the Triple Constraint 111

Understanding Quality in Projects 112

The Cost of Poor Quality 115

Balancing Cost and Quality 117

Common Cost & Quality Mistakes 119

Real-World Example: Building a House Budget & Quality Decisions 121

Connecting to Your Project (Project 1) 122

Full Steam Ahead - Process Port 125

End-of-Chapter Questions 126

Captain's Log: Discussion Board 127

Chapter 5 – Resource River 128

Entering Resource River 130

Understanding Project Resources 131

Roles and Responsibilities 132

Common Resource Management Mistakes 134

The Importance of Communication 135

Common Communication Challenges 137

Communication Is Not Just Talking 139

Real-World Example: Building a House Team & Communication 140

Connecting to Your Project (Project 1) 141

Full Steam Ahead - Process Port 144

End-of-Chapter Questions 145

Captain's Log: Discussion Board 146

Chapter 6 – Risky Rapids 147

⚓ Entering Risky Rapids 149

Understanding Risk in Projects 150

Types of Risk: Threats and Opportunities 151

Risk Identification 152

Risk Assessment (Likelihood & Impact) 154

Risk Response Strategies 156

Proactive vs. Reactive Risk Management 159

Common Risk Management Mistakes 160

Real-World Example: Building a House and Managing Risk
.... 161

Connecting to Your Project (Project 1) 162

Full Steam Ahead - Process Port 165

End-of-Chapter Questions 166

📓 Captain's Log: Discussion Board 167

Chapter 7 – Procurement Point 168

⚓ Arriving at Procurement Point 170

Understanding Procurement 170

Make-or-Buy Decisions 172

Understanding Contracts 174

Common Types of Contracts 175

Risks in Procurement 177

Managing Vendor Relationships 178

Common Procurement Mistakes 180

Real-World Example: Building a House and Working with
Vendors 182

Connecting to Your Project (Project 1) 183

Full Steam Ahead - Process Port 186

End-of-Chapter Questions.. 187

Captain's Log: Discussion Board 188

Chapter 8 - Planning Peninsula..189

Reaching Planning Peninsula 191

What Is a Project Management Plan? 191

Integrating the Plan Components 193

Alignment and Consistency 194

Identifying Gaps in the Plan................................... 194

The Role of Integration 195

Common Planning Mistakes 196

Connecting to Your Project (Project 1) 197

Full Steam Ahead - Process Port 199

End-of-Chapter Questions...................................... 200

Captain's Log: Discussion Board 201

Welcome Back.. 203

Project 2 – Project Experience...205

Purpose of This Project 205

Project 2 – Experience Log Checklist 212

Chapter 9 – PMI Island...213

Arriving at PMI Island.. 215

What Is PMI? 216

Understanding the PMBOK® Guide 217

Process Groups: The Project Lifecycle 218

Knowledge Areas: The Areas of Focus 220

How Process Groups and Knowledge Areas Work Together

.... 225

Connecting PMI to Your Project Management Plan 228

Real-World Example: Aligning a House Project with PMI
.... 230

Connecting to Your Project: Transition to Project 2........ 232

End-of-Chapter Questions.. 233

📓 Captain's Log: Discussion Board 234

Chapter 10 – Execution Bay...235

⚓ Entering Execution Bay 237

What Is Project Execution? 238

The Role of the Project Manager During Execution....... 239

Managing.. 242

Leading the Team 244

Communication During Execution.................................... 246

Handling Issues and Changes.. 248

Maintaining Alignment with the Plan 250

Common Execution Mistakes 252

Real-World Example: Executing a House Construction
Project... 253

Connecting to Your Project 2 254

Chapter 11 – Control Tower Waters.....................................258

⚓ Entering Control Tower Waters 260

What Is Monitoring and Controlling? 261

Planned vs. Actual Performance....................................... 263

Understanding Variance 264

Performance Measurement (Introducing Earned Value
Concepts).. 266

Earned Value Formula Visual.. 268

Managing Changes 268

Taking Corrective Action 270

Real-World Example: Monitoring a House Construction
Project 275

Connecting to Your Project 2 276

⚓ Key Takeaways 277

End-of-Chapter Questions 278

📓 Captain's Log: Discussion Board 278

Chapter 12 – Leadership Lookout 279

⚓ Entering Leadership Lookout 281

Leadership in Project Management 282

Organizational Structures and Leadership 284

Common Organizational Structures: 285

    Functional Organizations 285

    Matrix Organizations (Weak, Balanced, Strong) 286

    Projectized Organizations 287

Leadership Theories: Foundations of Understanding 288

Maslow's Hierarchy of Entrepreneurial Needs 289

McGregor's Theory X and Theory Y 292

McClelland's Needs Theory 295

Ethics in Leadership 298

Conscious Leadership 301

Limitations of Traditional Leadership Theories 302

Introducing Symbiotic Leadership 305

Symbiotic Leadership: Brings It All Together 312

Real-World Example: Leading a Project Team 315

Connecting to Your Project 2 315

End-of-Chapter Questions.. 317

📓 Captain's Log: Discussion Board 317

Chapter 13 – Agile Archipelago 318

⚓ Entering Agile Archipelago 320

What Is Agile?... 321

The Agile Manifesto.. 322

The 12 Principles Behind the Agile Manifesto 324

Agile in Practice: Iterative Delivery.............................. 326

Scrum Basics: A Practical Framework 328

Scrum Roles 328

Scrum Events... 329

Scrum Artifacts.. 330

Agile vs. Traditional Approaches 331

Traditional (Waterfall) Approach 331

Agile Approach 332

Where Agile Goes Wrong.. 332

Agile in the Real World... 335

Leadership in Agile Environments...................................... 336

Agile Lifecycle... 339

Real-World Example: Agile in Home Design 340

Connecting to Your Project 2 340

End-of-Chapter Questions.. 342

📓 Captain's Log: Discussion Board 342

Chapter 14 – Accountability 343

⚓ Entering Accountability Anchorage...................... 345

Responsibility vs. Accountability...................................... 346

What Is Accountability? 347

Accountability and Ownership...................................... 349

Accountability and Value Creation................................ 350

The Trickle-Down / Trickle-Up Value Loop 351

Trickle-Down Value Requirements 351

Trickle-Up Value Delivery 354

The Value Feedback Loop 356

What This Means for Accountability 358

Barriers to Accountability 360

Building a Culture of Accountability 361

Real-World Example: Applying the Value Loop to
Construction 364

Connecting to Your Project 2 364

End-of-Chapter Questions... 366

   Captain's Log: Discussion Board 366

Chapter 15 – Closing Dock...367

   Arriving at the Closing Dock...................................... 369

What Is Project Closure?... 370

Finalizing Deliverables 371

Administrative Closure 373

Lessons Learned.. 374

Knowledge Transfer 376

Common Closure Mistakes 377

Real-World Example: Closing a House Construction Project
.... 379

Connecting to Your Project 2 379

End-of-Chapter Questions 381

📕 Captain's Log: Discussion Board 381

Chapter 16 – The Finish Line 382

⚓ Reaching the Finish Line 384

Looking Back: The Full Journey 385

Project Management Beyond the Classroom 387

Continuous Improvement 389

Your Role Moving Forward 390

Real-World Example: Your First Project After This Course
.... 392

Connecting to Your Project 2 393

End-of-Chapter Questions 394

📕 Captain's Log: Discussion Board 396

Final Thought 396

Captain's Final Words 397

Glossary 398

Index 406

Dedication

This book is dedicated to the people who shaped my journey in project management and helped turn an interest into a calling.

To Dr. Angela Patrick, thank you for being the spark that started it all. Sitting in your class and hearing you speak about project management and the PMP certification changed the direction of my life. I would not be where I am today without your influence.

To Eric and Chrystal Haberman, thank you for your friendship, mentorship, and support from the very beginning. What began at one of my first PMI chapter meetings has become a lasting relationship that has guided me in more ways than one.

To the Project Management Institute (PMI), thank you for creating one of the most challenging and rewarding experiences of my career. Beyond the exam, you have built a global community where project managers can connect, grow, and realize they are part of something bigger.

Thank you,

Dr. Brian Haywood

Author Biography

Dr. Brian Haywood, DBA, PMP, is a seasoned project management professional, global technology leader, and college professor with extensive experience leading complex initiatives across multiple industries. He has successfully guided large-scale projects for Fortune 500 companies, working with global teams to deliver high-impact solutions in fast-paced, evolving environments.

In addition to his industry experience, Dr. Haywood teaches project management at colleges and universities, where he focuses on helping students translate theory into practical, real-world application. His teaching style emphasizes clarity, structure, and hands-on learning, equipping students with the skills needed to succeed in professional environments.

Dr. Haywood holds a Doctor of Business Administration (DBA) in Leadership and is a certified Project Management Professional (PMP®). His academic research has explored leadership transitions, organizational stability, and the role of trust in achieving successful outcomes. Through both his professional and academic work, he has developed a strong foundation in leadership, strategy, and execution.

He is also the creator of the Symbiotic Leadership™ framework, which emphasizes trust, accountability, and mutual growth within teams and organizations. His work bridges the gap between leadership theory and practical application, helping individuals and organizations achieve sustainable success.

Full Steam Ahead reflects Dr. Haywood's commitment to simplifying complex concepts and making project management accessible, engaging, and actionable for students, professionals, and aspiring leaders alike.

FULL STEAM AHEAD:
→ PROJECT MAP (1st HALF) ←
CHAPTER 8:
PLANNING
PENINSULA
N
W E
S
CHAPTER 7:
PROCUREMENT
POINT
CHAPTER 6:
RISKY
RAPIDS
CHAPTER 5:
RESOURCE
RIVER
CHAPTER 4:
COST & QUALITY
COVES
CHAPTER 3:
SCHEDULE
SHOALS
CHAPTER 2:
SCOPE
SHORES
DELIVERABLES
CHAPTER 1:
WELCOME
ABOARD

Introduction - Welcome Aboard

The river reflects the stillness of the morning, while the engines hum to life, ready for the adventure ahead. Crew members hustle on deck, each engaged in their tasks, contributing to the excitement of the journey to come. As preparations unfold, the atmosphere buzzes with anticipation for the voyage that lies ahead.

Welcome to Full Steam Ahead: A Simple Guide to Project Management.

Project management is a skill applicable in nearly every industry and profession. Whether someone is launching a product, organizing an event, implementing a new technology system, or planning a family vacation, they are managing a project. Projects are temporary efforts to produce something unique and need planning, coordination, communication, and leadership to succeed.

Many individuals experience project management through intricate frameworks and dense textbooks. This complexity can overshadow the discipline's true power. Consequently, the way it is often taught can make project management seem more challenging than it actually is.

This book takes a different approach.

Instead of presenting project management as a confusing jumble of terms and processes, this book takes you on a journey to understand it. Throughout the upcoming chapters, you'll learn the key principles of project management while imagining yourself as the captain of a riverboat navigating a long, winding waterway.

Each stop along the river symbolizes a key concept in project management. Some locations are peaceful harbors where plans are made, and resources are collected. Others are more challenging stretches of water where risks must be managed and decisions made carefully.

By the conclusion of this journey, you will gain a solid understanding of project management concepts. Additionally, you will create practical tools that showcase your skills. This experience will empower you to apply these concepts effectively in real-world scenarios.

What Makes This Book Different

Many textbooks focus mainly on theory. While understanding concepts is important, project management is primarily a practical skill. The best way to learn it is by applying it directly.

Therefore, this book centers around two major projects designed for you to complete as you read. These projects allow you to apply the concepts from each chapter in a structured way. By participating in these activities, you'll find the material more meaningful and relevant to your learning experience.

Project 1: The Project Management Plan Project

In the first half of this book, you'll create a complete Project Management Plan for a project of your choice. As you move through Chapters 1 to 8, each chapter will help you develop a different part of the plan. By the end of Chapter 8, you'll have built a comprehensive project plan similar to those used by professional project managers.

This project will help you understand the importance of planning activities. By defining the scope, creating schedules, estimating costs, and identifying risks, you can better manage a project's complexities. Additionally, effectively organizing stakeholders is essential for guiding the project toward success.

Project 2: The Project Experience Project

The second half of the book focuses on a skill that many students only recognize they need later in their careers, which is how to properly document their project management experience. Organizations such as the Project Management Institute (PMI) require professionals seeking certifications, such as the Project Management Professional (PMP), to record their experience across five process groups:

- Initiating
- Planning
- Executing
- Monitoring and Controlling
- Closing

Throughout Chapters 9 through 16, you will begin the process of building your own Project Experience Log. This exercise is designed to help you recognize how your everyday work activities relate to formal project management processes and methodologies. As you engage in this activity, you will likely uncover insights that highlight how your routine tasks align with established project management principles.

Many students discover that they already possess valuable project experience, even if they haven't yet learned to express it in the terms commonly used in project management. This realization can be quite enlightening, as it allows you to see the relevance of your past roles and responsibilities in a new light. By framing your experiences in project management terminology, you enhance the value of your skills and knowledge.

By completing this exercise, you will not only organize your professional experiences but also prepare for future certification applications. This preparation is essential in demonstrating your skills and understanding of project management concepts to certifying bodies. Ultimately, keeping a detailed Project Experience Log will greatly support your career growth and progression in project management.

What You Will Learn

The upcoming chapters will guide you through the key stages of project management. In the first part of the book, you will learn how to plan a project effectively. This includes setting goals, identifying stakeholders, creating schedules, estimating costs, managing risks, and organizing resources.

In the second half of the book, you will examine how projects are executed, monitored, and finished. You will also gain insights into leadership, accountability, agile project methods, and professional project management standards. Together, these topics offer a practical foundation for understanding how to deliver successful projects.

How to Get the Most from This Book

The book promotes active involvement by offering various exercises in every chapter. These tasks are designed to help you grasp and implement the concepts more effectively. Engaging with the activities will improve your understanding and solidify your knowledge, enriching your learning experience.

To get the most from this experience:

- Choose a project idea that interests you.
- Take time to complete the exercises in each chapter.
- Revisit earlier sections as your understanding grows.
- Think about how the concepts apply to real situations you have encountered.

Project management is a skill that improves with experience. Actively engaging with the material deepens your understanding and refines your techniques. The more you practice, the more valuable your expertise becomes in real-world situations.

The Journey Ahead

As you progress through the chapters, picture yourself journeying along a winding river full of chances to learn new skills and face new challenges. Some parts of the water will be calm and easy, while others may need careful steering and wise choices. However, just as a well-managed voyage becomes simpler when the crew knows the plan and the captain remains focused on the path ahead, reaching the destination becomes simpler when the crew knows the plan and the captain remains focused on the path ahead.

The engines are ready.

The river awaits.

Let's get underway.

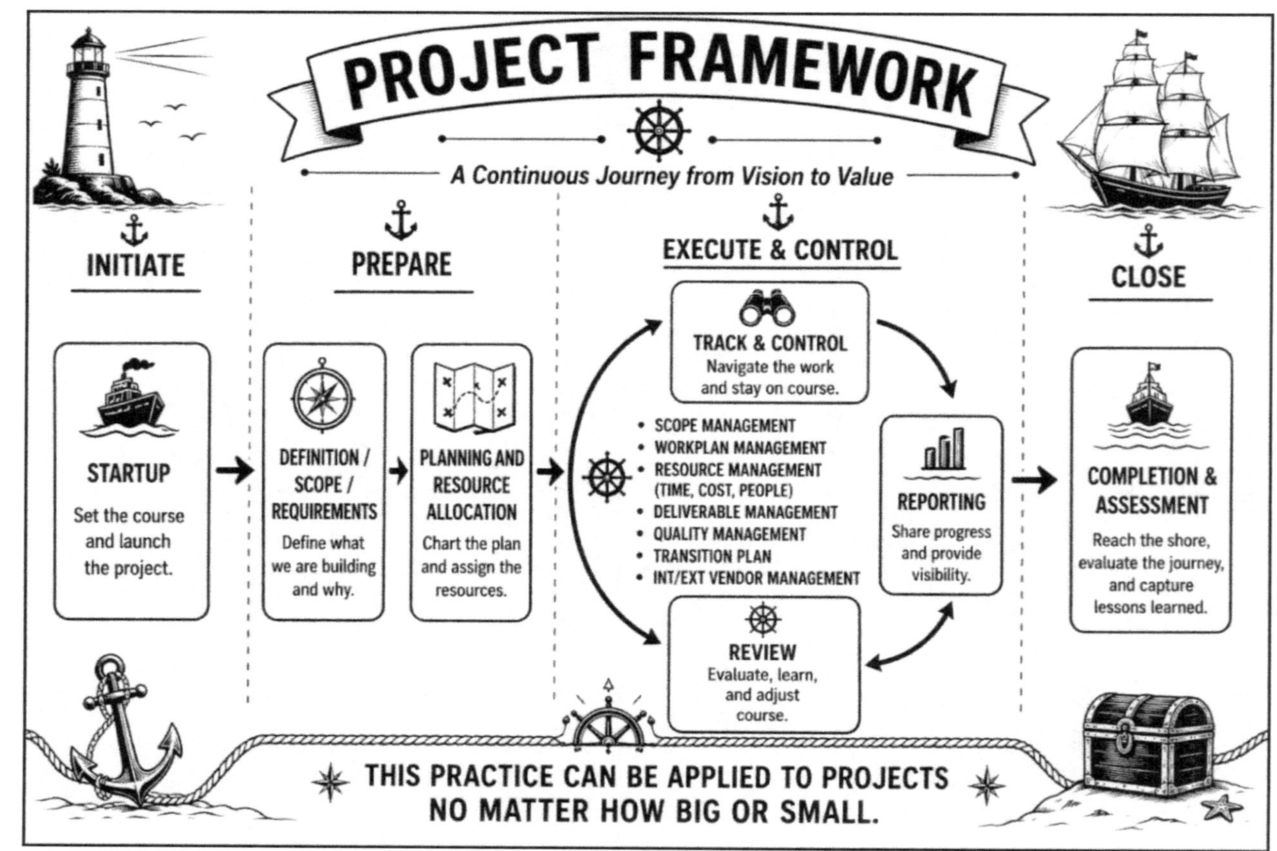

PROJECT FRAMEWORK
A Continuous Journey from Vision to Value
INITIATE
PREPARE
EXECUTE & CONTROL
CLOSE
STARTUP
Set the course and launch the project.
DEFINITION / SCOPE / REQUIREMENTS
Define what we are building and why.
PLANNING AND RESOURCE ALLOCATION
Chart the plan and assign the resources.
TRACK & CONTROL
Navigate the work and stay on course.
SCOPE MANAGEMENT
WORKPLAN MANAGEMENT
RESOURCE MANAGEMENT (TIME, COST, PEOPLE)
DELIVERABLE MANAGEMENT
QUALITY MANAGEMENT
TRANSITION PLAN
INT/EXT VENDOR MANAGEMENT
REPORTING
Share progress and provide visibility.
REVIEW
Evaluate, learn, and adjust course.
COMPLETION & ASSESSMENT
Reach the shore, evaluate the journey, and capture lessons learned.
THIS PRACTICE CAN BE APPLIED TO PROJECTS NO MATTER HOW BIG OR SMALL.

Project 1 - The Project Management Plan

Every successful journey starts with thorough planning. Before setting sail, the captain and crew need to know their destination, the route, necessary supplies, and possible hazards. Without proper preparation, even the sturdiest ship can go off course. Similarly, projects require careful planning to succeed.

In the first half of this book, you will embark on the journey of constructing a complete Project Management Plan tailored to a project of your choosing. Each chapter, from 1 to 8, is designed to guide you systematically in developing a specific component of your plan. This structured approach will ensure you gain a comprehensive understanding of the elements of effective project management.

By the conclusion of Chapter 8, you will have assembled a well-organized project plan that mirrors those used by professional project managers across organizations worldwide. This hands-on project planning experience will not only enhance your learning but also provide you with a practical framework to apply in real-world scenarios. You will be equipped with valuable insights that go beyond theoretical knowledge.

As you work through this project, you will practice using the tools and thinking processes that seasoned project managers employ every day. This practical application is essential for developing the skills needed to manage projects successfully. Ultimately, this book aims to bridge the gap between theory and practice, giving you the confidence to tackle real-life project management challenges.

Choosing Your Project

The first step is to choose a project you will use throughout the planning part of this book. Your project should be realistic and interesting to you. It doesn't need to be very complex, but it should include multiple activities, stakeholders, and resources.

Examples of possible projects include:

- Launching a small business or online store

- Planning a community event or fundraiser

- Developing a mobile application

- Organizing a conference or workshop

- Creating a marketing campaign

- Planning a wedding or large celebration

You will begin by identifying two or three possible project ideas and briefly describing each one.

For each idea, consider the following questions:

Project Overview: What is the project?

Project Purpose: Why is this project being undertaken? What problem does it solve or value does it create?

Expected Deliverables: What will exist once the project is successfully completed?

After reviewing your ideas, you will select one project to develop throughout the remainder of this exercise.

Building Your Project Management Plan

A Project Management Plan is a collection of documents that guide how a project will be executed, monitored, and completed. It describes the scope of the project, the schedule, the resources required, the risks involved, and how communication will occur among stakeholders.

Throughout Chapters 1 through 8, you will build the following components of your plan.

Business Case

The **Business Case** outlines the rationale behind the project's existence. It offers a concise justification for the investment and helps stakeholders grasp the anticipated benefits. By presenting these insights, the Business Case ensures that everyone involved understands the project's value.

For this section, you will describe:

- The project idea

- The purpose of the project

- The expected value or outcome once the project is complete

Figure 1.1 Example Business Case

Business Case: Residential Home Construction

Prepared By: Your name Goes Here (generic placeholder, matching <image1> and <image 1])

1. Executive Summary: The high-level overview justification paragraph for building a new custom home [in inesidorotal inesiduation] standard, succeeds and prroject.

2. Problem Statement: Pre-existing pre-owned homes are not suitable. Tsjjiely, hidden costs, holden adote highly hidden costs or custom tailored funces, lack of custom tailored functionality for flood comstibilty for 3-bed, 2-bath layout,

3. Business Opportunity: Explaining the potential for financial gain and more custom lifestyle standard and cool custom lifestyle atford building commaestions, through custom design and new construction [tnd new construction.

4. Options Analysis: High-level view showing that Option B offers inrein comparing home option over final

Option A: Purchase Pre-existing Home	**Option B:** Custom Design and New
Option B: Custom Design and New Construction	Defined control over final home standard and costs compared and costs.

5. High-Level Financial Assessment: alu [cite: 1]:

Total Estimated Investment: ~$255,000 [cite: (e construction of the specified 3-bedroom, 2-bathroom home), soft costs, and high-level Contingency fund.	**Post-Construction Home Valuation Estimate**	~$320,000
	Estimated ROI	~25%

**Note: figures are slightly higher than thin final charter construction budget : total soft costs and pre-charter contingency.*

7. Recommendation:
A recommendenerd to approval to proceed with formalizing the customized home construction option via Project Charter [cite: 1]. (The document continues proemly to authorization, the document continus seamlessly to authorization)

Proceed with Project Charter Authorization: [cite: MM/DD/YYYY]
Approval / Signature Line
Project Sponsor signature:

The ***Project Charter*** serves as the official document that grants permission for a project to commence. It outlines the project manager's authority and clarifies the project's high-level scope. This essential document sets the foundation for project planning and execution.

Your Project Charter should include:

- Project Name

- Project Scope (High-Level Description)

- Estimated Project Schedule

- Estimated Budget

- Project Manager

Example project names might include:

- Project Red Lightning

- Project Serenity

- Build a Backyard Shed

- Winter Vacation Plan

The charter does not need to be overly detailed. It simply establishes the project's initial direction.

Figure 1.2 Example Project Charter

Example Project Charter

Project Name: Residential Home Construction

Project Objective:
Construct a single-family, 3-bedroom, 2-bathroom residential home within a defined budget and schedule, meeting quality and safety standards.

High-Level Scope:
Design and construct a fully functional residential home, including foundation, structure, electrical, plumbing, and interior finishing.

Key Stakeholders:
- Homeowner (Client)
- Project Manager
- General Contractor
- Subcontractors (Electrical, Plumbing, HVAC)
- Local Inspectors

Estimated Schedule:
- Estimated: ~ 21 weeks

Estimated Budget:
- Estimated: $230,000

Project Manager:
- Your name Goes Here (Gives you Authority)

Stakeholder Register

Projects rarely happen in isolation because they usually involve various individuals and groups who can be impacted by the project's outcome. The ***Stakeholder Register*** is an essential tool that identifies these people or organizations. This ensures that those who may influence or be affected by the project are recognized and their interests taken into account.

The Stakeholder Register is considered a living document, meaning it is continually updated as the project advances. As new stakeholders are identified during planning, their information can be added. This flexibility enables a more comprehensive understanding of the project's social landscape.

Examples of stakeholders might include:

- Team members

- Customers

- Sponsors

- Vendors

- Supervisors

- Family members (for personal projects)

As you continue planning your project, you will add stakeholders to this register.

Stakeholder Matrix

Once your Stakeholder Register is complete, you will develop a Power–Interest Matrix. This matrix helps project managers understand the influence of different stakeholders and their level of interest in the project's outcome. Recognizing this relationship helps determine how often stakeholders should receive updates and which communication methods to use.

Figure 1.3 Stakeholder Matrix

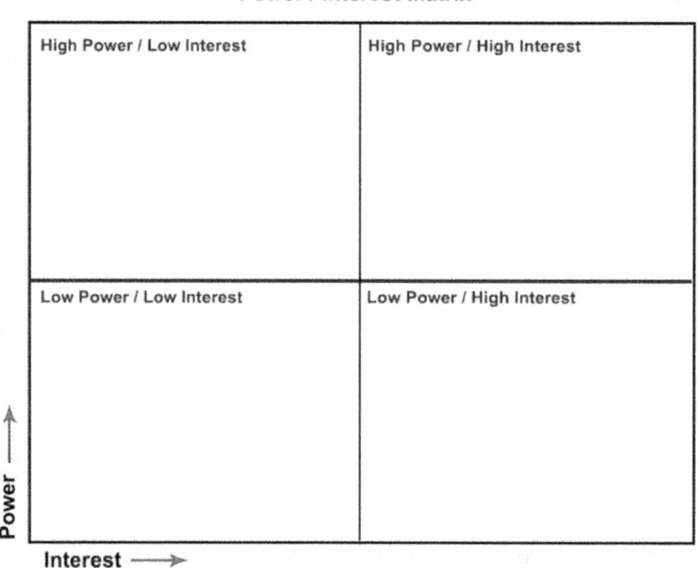

Requirements Document

A Requirements Document identifies the conditions or capabilities needed for the project to succeed.

Requirements describe what must be true in order for the project deliverables to be considered complete.

For example, if the project involves planning a vacation, requirements might include:

- The trip must occur between specific dates

- The destination must include family-friendly activities

- Hotel rooms must accommodate all travelers

- Transportation must be available

The Requirements Document is an essential tool in project management. Similar to the Stakeholder Register, it is a live document. As the project progresses, this document can expand and adapt to include more detailed planning. Keeping it current ensures that all stakeholder needs are accurately represented throughout the project lifecycle.

Project Scope Statement (Scope Baseline)

The Project Scope Statement outlines the project's boundaries and details the work to be done. It plays a key role in preventing unnecessary expansion of project goals. Clearly specifying what is included and what is not helps set expectations for all stakeholders.

Your initial scope statement will build upon the information provided in your Project Charter. As the planning process continues, you may refine this scope to ensure it aligns with project requirements. This iterative refinement helps more accurately address stakeholder expectations.

This initial scope becomes your Scope Baseline, which serves as the project's reference point. It allows you to compare the original project definition with the final project scope. Once planning is complete, this comparison is crucial for assessing project changes and performance.

Activity List

To create a schedule, you must first identify the activities needed to complete the project. Make a list of the main activities required to meet your project deliverables. The list doesn't need to include every minor step, but it should include the key tasks necessary to finish the project.

Figure 1.4 Example Activity List

Activities List

	Activity	Predecessor	Duration (days)
A1	Draw BluePrint	START	7
A2	Dig Earth	A1	3
A3	Get Materials, labor	A1	1
A4	Lay Foundation	A2, A3	5
B1	Get Materials	A4	3
B2	Construct Pillars & Beams	B1	10
B3	Finish Plumbing	B4, B5	3
B4	Construct Walls	B2	3
B5	Finish Electrical/ Cable Work	B2	3
C1	Design Interiors	START	3
C2	Decide Furniture	C1	2
C3	Decide Light Fixtures	C2	1
C4	Procure Furniture	C3	3
C5	Procure Light Fixtures	C3	3
C6	Fix Lights, AC and fans	C4, C5, B3	5
D1	Design Private Public Areas	START	5
D2	Lay Walkways	D1	7
D3	Set up lawns	D2	4
D4	Plant saplings	D3	2
Total Days			73

Network Diagram

After identifying the activities in your project, the next step is to determine the order in which they should be performed. It's important to recognize that some activities depend on others being completed first; for example, if Task A cannot start until Task B is finished, this dependency must be included in your plan. Additionally, some tasks may be done simultaneously, which can help save time and resources.

A Network Diagram is a valuable tool for clearly visualizing dependencies and activity order. This diagram shows the relationships between tasks, indicating which activities follow others and how they connect within the workflow. Using a Network Diagram allows project managers to fully understand how tasks move from start to finish. This clarity improves scheduling, helps identify potential bottlenecks, and streamlines project execution.

Critical Path

In a project's network diagram, the Critical Path highlights the sequence of dependent activities that determine the shortest possible project duration. These tasks are essential because they directly influence the overall schedule; a delay in any activity on this path will postpone the project's completion.

Understanding and identifying the critical path allows project managers to prioritize their resources and efforts on these time-sensitive tasks, ensuring that they are completed on schedule. By monitoring these activities closely and managing potential risks that could delay the project, project managers can effectively safeguard the project timeline and enhance the overall efficiency of project execution.

Figure 1.5 Example Network Diagram

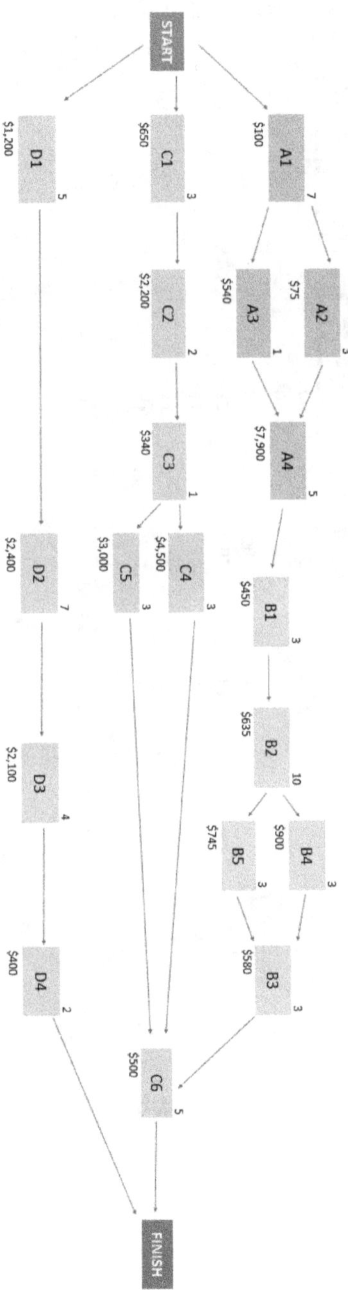

Figure 1.6 Example Critical Path

Path 1	.	Path 2	..	Path 3	...	Path 4	....	Path 5	.....	Path 6		Path 7	
A1	7	A1	7	A1	7	A1	7	C1	3	C1	3	D1	5
A2	3	A2	3	A3	1	A3	1	C2	2	C2	2	D2	7
A4	5	A4	5	A4	5	A4	5	C3	1	C3	1	D3	4
B1	3	B1	3	B1	3	B1	3	C4	3	C5	3	D4	2
B2	10	B2	10	B2	10	B2	10	C6	5	C6	5		
B4	3	B5	3	B4	3	B5	3						
B3	3	B3	3	B3	3	B3	3						
C6	5	C6	5	C6	5	C6	5						
Total	39		39		37		37		14		14		18

Activity Cost Estimates

Every activity outlined in your project is likely to incur specific costs that need to be meticulously accounted for. These costs can encompass a variety of categories, including labor expenses for personnel involved, materials required to complete tasks, outsourced services, and equipment that must be acquired or rented.

To effectively manage your project budget, it's essential to estimate the costs for each activity in your activity list. Carefully break down the cost components for each task, including hourly labor rates, material quantities and prices, external service charges, and any necessary equipment fees. This thorough approach will provide a clear financial framework to guide your project execution.

Activity Cost with ROM (Cost Baseline)

After evaluating and estimating the costs for each activity in the project, the next step is to combine these costs into a total. At this point, it is important to include a Range of Magnitude (ROM) percentage in your calculations. This ROM percentage serves as a safety margin to account for potential risks, uncertainties, and unforeseen expenses that may arise during project execution.

Including a buffer in project planning is essential, as it acknowledges the uncertainty in defining or predicting all variables at the project's onset. By incorporating the ROM percentage, you can create a more accurate financial outlook. This approach helps address the natural variability inherent in project management.

The final output of this process is called the Cost Baseline. It represents the total expected expenditure to complete the project, covering the estimated costs of specific activities and a buffer for risk management. During the project's lifecycle, the Cost Baseline serves as a reference point for monitoring the budget and evaluating financial progress, helping keep the project on track toward its financial objectives.

Figure 1.7 Example Activity Cost with ROM

Activities List

	Activity	Cost Baseline	Est %	Level of Accuracy ($$$)	Predecessor	Schedule Baseline	ROM	Level of Accuracy (Days)
A1	Draw BluePrint	$ 100	20%	$ 120.00	START	7	20%	8
A2	Dig Earth	$ 75.00	20%	$ 90.00	A1	3	20%	4
A3	Get Materials, labor	$ 540.00	20%	$ 648.00	A1	1	20%	1
A4	Lay Foundation	$ 900.00	20%	$ 1,080.00	A2, A3	5	20%	6
B1	Get Materials	$ 450.00	20%	$ 540.00	A4	3	20%	4
B2	Construct Pillars & Beams	$ 635.00	20%	$ 762.00	B1	10	20%	12
B3	Finish Plumbing	$ 580.00	20%	$ 696.00	B4, B5	3	20%	4
B4	Construct Walls	$ 900.00	20%	$ 1,080.00	B2	3	20%	4
B5	Finish Electrical/ Cable Work	$ 745.00	20%	$ 894.00	B2	3	20%	4
C1	Design Interiors	$ 650.00	20%	$ 780.00	START	3	20%	4
C2	Decide Furniture	$ 2,200.00	20%	$ 2,640.00	C1	2	20%	2
C3	Decide Light Fixtures	$ 340.00	20%	$ 408.00	C2	1	20%	1
C4	Procure Furniture	$ 4,500.00	20%	$ 5,400.00	C3	3	20%	4
C5	Procure Light Fixtures	$ 3,000.00	20%	$ 3,600.00	C3	3	20%	4
C6	Fix Lights, AC and fans	$ 500.00	20%	$ 600.00	C4, C5, B3	5	20%	6
D1	Design Private Public Areas	$ 1,200.00	20%	$ 1,440.00	START	5	20%	6
D2	Lay Walkways	$ 2,400.00	20%	$ 2,880.00	D1	7	20%	8
D3	Set up lawns	$ 2,100.00	20%	$ 2,520.00	D2	4	20%	5
D4	Plant saplings	$ 400.00	20%	$ 480.00	D3	2	20%	2
		$ 22,215.00	20%	$ 26,658.00		73	20%	88

Quality Metrics

Quality metrics serve as critical benchmarks for evaluating whether a project's outputs align with predefined expectations and standards. These metrics are derived from the project's Scope and Requirements, providing a structured approach to assessing quality. The specific quality metrics used can vary significantly depending on the nature and type of the project. Common examples of these factors might include:

- **Performance Metrics**: Evaluating how well the deliverables function in terms of efficiency, speed, and reliability.
- **Compliance Metrics**: Ensuring that the project meets all relevant regulatory, safety, and industry standards.
- **Customer Satisfaction**: Measuring user feedback and satisfaction levels through surveys or user testing.
- **Defect Density**: Assessing the number of defects found in the deliverables relative to the size or complexity of the project components.
- **Timeliness**: Monitoring whether the deliverables were completed on schedule and identifying any delays in the project timeline.
- **Cost Effectiveness**: Analyzing whether the project stayed within budget and the value received for the investment made.

By closely tracking these metrics throughout the project lifecycle, teams can confirm they are moving toward meeting quality standards and can make informed adjustments as needed to enhance overall project results. Consider how you will evaluate if your project has achieved the desired quality level.

Team Roles and Responsibilities

In project management, recognizing the importance of coordinated efforts among team members is essential for successful project completion. Each team member should have specific roles and responsibilities, and to promote clarity and efficiency, it is crucial to create a comprehensive list detailing all team members and their respective duties.

By defining these roles, even in a hypothetical project, you can gain a better understanding of how tasks will be organized and how team members will collaborate. This clarity is vital for setting expectations and ensuring that everyone is aligned with the project's goals.

Preferred Communication Methods

Different stakeholders often have varying preferences for how they receive information. Some may favor face-to-face meetings, while others might prefer emails or virtual presentations. It's important to accommodate these diverse communication styles to ensure effective collaboration.

Examples include: Email, Phone calls, Messaging applications, Video meetings, In-person discussions.

Your communication plan should outline how information will be shared with stakeholders throughout the project.

Figure 1.8 Preferred Communication Plan

THE PROJECT VOYAGE COMMUNICATION PLAN: KEEPING THE VOYAGE ON COURSE

STAKEHOLDER	FREQUENCY	METHOD
Homeowner	Weekly	Status meetings
Contractor Team	Daily	On-site briefings
Vendors	As needed	Email / Calls
Inspectors	Milestone-based	scheduled visits

Risk Register

Every project naturally involves some uncertainty due to factors such as scope changes, resource availability, or external environmental influences. To manage this uncertainty effectively, a Risk Register is an essential tool that systematically identifies potential risks, events, or conditions that could harm the project's goals, schedule, or budget.

This register not only catalogs identified risks but also assesses their potential impact and likelihood of occurrence, enabling project managers to prioritize and develop mitigation strategies. By maintaining and regularly updating a Risk Register, teams can better prepare for challenges and increase the project's overall resilience.

Examples of risks might include:

- Budget overruns

- Resource shortages

- Schedule delays

- Vendor issues

When a risk is identified, it should be added to the Risk Register.

Figure 1.9 Example Risk Register

THE PROJECT VOYAGE RISK REGISTER: NAVIGATING POTENTIAL OBSTACLES

RISK	IMPACT	MITIGATION
Weather delays	High	Build buffer into schedule
Material shortages	Medium	Pre-order materials early
Labor availability	Medium	Secure contracts in advance
Cost overruns	High	Monitor budget regularly
Inspection delays	Low	Schedule inspections early

Risk Responses

For each identified risk, it is essential to evaluate response strategies to mitigate potential negative impacts. Possible strategies may include risk avoidance, where actions are taken to eliminate the risk altogether. Additionally, implementing risk transfer methods, such as insurance, can be an effective way to manage risks that cannot be completely avoided.

Examples of responses include:

- Avoid the risk

- Reduce the likelihood of the risk

- Transfer the risk to another party

- Accept the risk and monitor it

You don't need to provide a detailed quantitative risk analysis for this exercise, but you should think about the potential impact of each risk and possible ways to address it.

Procurement Planning

Some projects require external vendors to supply specific goods or services vital to the project's success. When your project involves such vendors, it's crucial to create a detailed Procurement Statement of Work (SOW). This document should clearly define the expectations, deliverables, timelines, and quality standards for the products or services vendors are expected to provide.

Along with the SOW, it is crucial to establish clear source selection criteria. These criteria will help you evaluate and choose potential vendors based on factors such as experience, reliability, cost-effectiveness, and the quality of their offerings. Having a structured vendor selection process not only supports making informed decisions but also ensures that the chosen vendors align well with your project's goals and requirements.

Examples of criteria include:

- Cost

- Availability

- Experience

- Licensing or certifications

- Geographic location

Additionally, consider whether certain work should be performed internally or purchased from external providers, a decision commonly known as the make-or-buy analysis.

Final Deliverable

At the end of Chapter 8, you'll compile all these components into a detailed Project Management Plan. This plan will demonstrate your understanding of the planning processes used in professional project management and will serve as the main deliverable for the first half of this book.

Project Plan Tasks Check-off List:

▉ Project Selection

☐ Identify 2–3 project ideas

☐ Describe the project overview for each

☐ Describe the project purpose for each

☐ Describe the expected deliverables for each

☐ Select final project (feeds into your Business Case)

▉ Initiation

Business Case

☐ Refine project overview

☐ Refine project purpose

☐ Refine expected deliverables

Project Charter

☐ Create project name

☐ Define high-level scope

☐ Define estimated schedule

☐ Define estimated budget

☐ Identify project manager

Stakeholder Register

- ☐ Identify initial stakeholders

- ☐ List stakeholder roles or interests

- ☐ Begin stakeholder register (living document)

Scope Planning

Requirements Document

- ☐ Identify initial requirements

- ☐ Add constraints and conditions

- ☐ Continue updating requirements (living document)

Scope Statement

- ☐ Draft initial scope statement

- ☐ Define what is included in the project

- ☐ Establish scope baseline

Schedule Planning

Activity List

- ☐ List major project activities

Activity Sequencing

- ☐ Identify dependencies between activities

Network Diagram

☐ Create network diagram

Critical Path

☐ Identify critical path

Cost Planning

Cost Estimates

☐ Assign cost to each activity

Budget

☐ Calculate total project cost (BAC)

☐ Establish cost baseline

Quality Planning

☐ Define quality metrics

☐ Identify how success will be measured

Resource Planning

☐ Identify team members or roles

☐ Define roles and responsibilities

Communication Planning

☐ Identify stakeholders' communication preferences

☐ Define communication methods

☐ Create a basic communication plan

Risk Planning

Risk Register

☐ Identify potential risks

☐ Document risks in the register

Risk Responses

☐ Define response strategy for each risk

Procurement Planning *(if applicable)*

☐ Define procurement needs

☐ Create statement of work (SOW)

☐ Define vendor selection criteria

☐ Identify make-or-buy considerations

Stakeholder Analysis

☐ Complete stakeholder register

☐ Create power–interest matrix

▊ Final Deliverable

☐ Compile all sections into one document

☐ Review for completeness

☐ Ensure alignment across all sections

☐ Submit final Project Management Plan

⦿ *Captain's Reminder*

A good plan isn't created overnight; it develops gradually. Stay consistent, stick to the process, and by the end of Chapter 8, you'll have something most students never achieve: a comprehensive, professional project plan.

Final Submission Checklist

Compile all components of your Project Management Plan into a single, organized document.

	Business Case - Identify 2–3 project ideas
	Project Charter
	Stakeholder Register
	Stakeholder Matrix
	Requirements Document
	Project Scope Statement
	Activity List
	Network Diagram
	Critical Path
	Activity Cost Estimates
	Project Cost Baseline
	Quality Metrics
	Team Member List (Roles and Responsibilities)
	Preferred Communication
	Risk Register
	Risk Responses
	Procurement Source Selection Criteria
	Procurement Statement of Work (SOW)
	Make-or-buy decision

Chapter 1 – Welcome Aboard

(Intro to Project Management)

☉ *Learning Objectives*

By the end of this chapter, you should be able to:

- ✓ Understand what project management is and why it matters
- ✓ Identify the role and responsibilities of a project manager
- ✓ Recognize the key phases of a project lifecycle
- ✓ Explain how project management applies beyond formal projects
- ✓ Describe the value of structure, planning, and leadership in projects

CHAPTER 1

Welcome Aboard

⚓ *A Journey Begins*

The early morning fog hung low across the river as the crew gathered along the dock. The paddlewheel boat sat quietly against the wooden pier, its polished brass fittings catching the first rays of sunlight. Smoke gently rose from the stack as the engine warmed below deck.

Captain Brian stood at the helm reviewing the chart laid out before him. The map showed a long, winding river with many turns, rapids, islands, and safe harbors along the way. Each point along the river represented a destination the crew would reach together. But before the journey could begin, one important question had to be answered.

Where exactly are we going?

Every successful voyage begins with a clear destination. The same is true for projects. Projects are everywhere. Businesses launch new products, companies upgrade technology systems, communities organize events, and families plan vacations. Behind each of these efforts is a project, a temporary endeavor undertaken to create something new.

Projects don't succeed by chance. Similar to a river journey, they need planning, leadership, communication, and careful steering. Without a clear plan, even a skilled team can lose their way. Unexpected obstacles may arise, resources can be depleted, and reaching the goal becomes more difficult.

Project management serves as the guide for the journey. In this book, you'll assume the role of a project manager steering a voyage from beginning to end. You'll learn how to set objectives, organize tasks, allocate resources, handle risks, and lead your team to success. Like the crew on this riverboat, you'll not just watch the journey but take an active part in it.

The Voyage You Are About to Begin

This book is designed to be both practical and interactive. Rather than only reading about project management concepts, you will build something real as you progress through the chapters.

By the time you reach the end of the first half of this book, you will have created a complete Project Management Plan for a project of your choosing. Each chapter will guide you in building a different section of that plan.

In the second half of the book, you will begin documenting your Project Management Experience. This exercise will help you understand how your work activities align with the project management process groups used by the Project Management Institute (PMI). Many students find this exercise especially valuable because it helps prepare them for professional certifications such as the Project Management Professional (PMP).

By the end of this journey, you will not only understand project management but also have produced real artifacts that demonstrate your skills.

What Is a Project?

Before our voyage continues, we need to first understand what a project truly is. A project is a temporary effort undertaken to produce a unique product, service, or outcome. Unlike ongoing operations, projects have a definite start and finish. They aim to achieve a specific goal.

Examples of projects include:

- Launching a new product

- Implementing a new software system

- Organizing a conference or event

- Building a website

- Planning a wedding

- Expanding a business to a new location

Each initiative has a specific goal, deadline, and necessary resources. The project manager is responsible for effectively managing these efforts.

Projects vs. Operations

Not all work qualifies as a project. It's essential to distinguish between projects and operations. A project is temporary and aims to produce a unique outcome, while an operation is continuous and repetitive.

For example:

- A project: Launching a new website

- An operation: Maintaining that website over time

- A project: Planning a wedding

- An operation: Managing a household

- A project: Developing a new product

- An operation: Producing that product repeatedly

Projects have:

- A clear beginning and end

- A defined goal

- Unique outcomes

Operations have:

- No defined end date

- Repetitive tasks

- Ongoing support of the business

Understanding this distinction helps you identify what work qualifies as project experience.

The Five Process Groups

Every project, regardless of size or industry, follows a similar structure. Project management is commonly organized into five process groups:

Initiating: Defining the project and gaining approval to begin

Planning: Creating the roadmap for how the project will be completed

Executing: Performing the work to complete the project

Monitoring and Controlling: Tracking progress and adjusting as needed

Closing: Finalizing the project and delivering the outcome

These process groups are not always linear; they often overlap and interact throughout the life of a project.

Throughout this book, you will work through each process group step by step. Think of them as phases of your journey along the river.

Project Constraints

Every project has boundaries. No matter how thoroughly a project is planned, there are always limits that influence what can be accomplished. These restrictions are called **project constraints**, and they affect every decision a project manager makes.

At the core of project management are three primary constraints: **scope, schedule, and cost**. These are often referred to as the **Triple Constraint**. Scope defines what work will be completed, schedule determines how long the work will take, and cost represents the resources required to complete the project. These three elements are closely connected, meaning that a change in one will almost always impact the others.

For example, expanding a project's scope by incorporating new features or requirements may lead to increased time or funding needs. Shortening the schedule to meet an earlier deadline might require additional resources, raising costs. Conversely, a reduced budget could force the team to scale down scope or extend the timeline. Project managers must consistently balance these competing demands to ensure the project stays aligned with its objectives.

While scope, schedule, and cost are the primary constraints, modern project management also recognizes additional constraints that influence project success. These include quality, resources, and risk. Quality ensures that the deliverables meet expectations and standards outlined in the scope. Resources refer to the people, tools, and materials available to complete the work. Risk represents the uncertainty that could affect the project's outcome.

These constraints form a network of interconnected factors that need careful management. A skilled project manager recognizes that enhancing one aspect often comes at the expense of others. Instead of considering constraints as mere obstacles, they should be viewed as helpful guides that help create feasible plans and make well-informed choices.

Figure 1.1.1 Triple Constraints

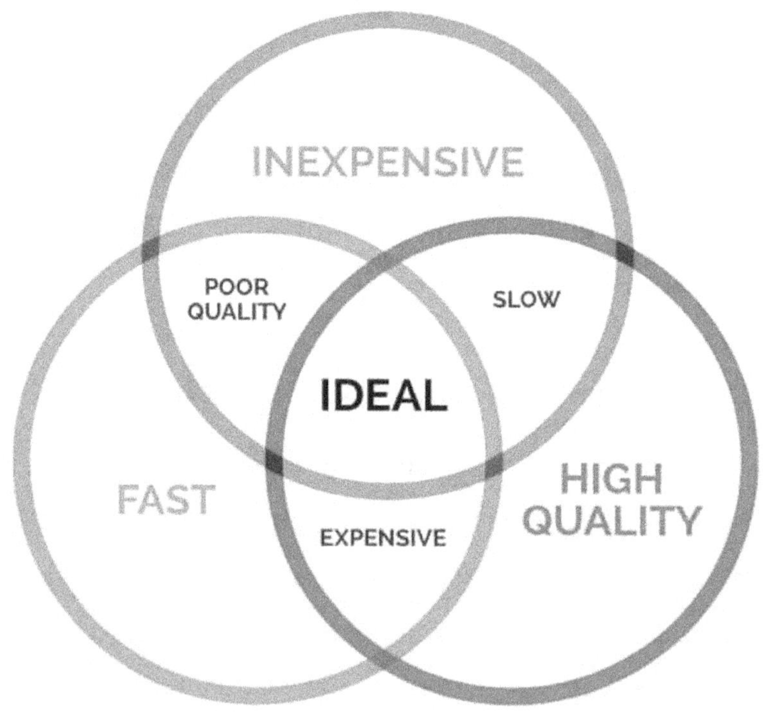

The Role of the Project Manager

The project manager acts much like the captain of a vessel. While the crew performs many individual tasks, the captain is responsible for keeping the entire journey on the right track. The captain ensures the destination is clear, the route is mapped, the crew understands their roles, and the ship stays on course when conditions change.

Similarly, the project manager coordinates people, resources, schedules, and expectations to guide the project toward completion. This role requires more than technical knowledge. Successful project managers rely on communication, leadership, problem-solving, and adaptability. They must anticipate obstacles and make decisions when circumstances change. As you progress through this book, you will begin developing the skills needed to perform this role effectively.

Why Project Management Matters

Project management is not limited to people with the title "Project Manager." It is a skill used in nearly every profession. Whether you work in:

- Business

- Technology

- Healthcare

- Education

- Retail

You are likely already involved in projects. Employers value individuals who can:

- Organize work

- Communicate effectively

- Manage time and resources

- Deliver results

These are all project management skills. Learning project management gives you a competitive advantage, regardless of your career path.

Professional Alignment

This chapter introduces foundational concepts used in professional project management standards.

- **PMI Talent Triangle**: Technical Project Management

- **Process Groups Introduced**: Initiating, Planning, Executing, Monitoring & Controlling, Closing

- **Knowledge Areas**: High-level awareness across all areas

These concepts will be expanded throughout the book as you continue your journey.

Choosing Your Project

Every voyage needs a destination. For your first assignment, you will begin identifying the project you would like to build a Project Management Plan for throughout this book. Think of something realistic and interesting to you. The project does not have to be large or complex, but it should involve multiple steps and stakeholders.

Examples might include:

- Launching a small online business

- Planning a charity fundraiser

- Creating a mobile application

- Organizing a community event

- Developing a marketing campaign

Choose two or three possible project ideas and briefly describe them. For each idea, answer the following questions:

Project Overview: What is the project?

Project Purpose: Why is this project being undertaken? What problem does it solve or value does it create?

Expected Deliverables: What will exist once the project is successfully completed?

In the next chapter, you will select one of these ideas and begin building your Project Charter, the official document that authorizes your project to begin.

Full Steam Ahead - Process Port

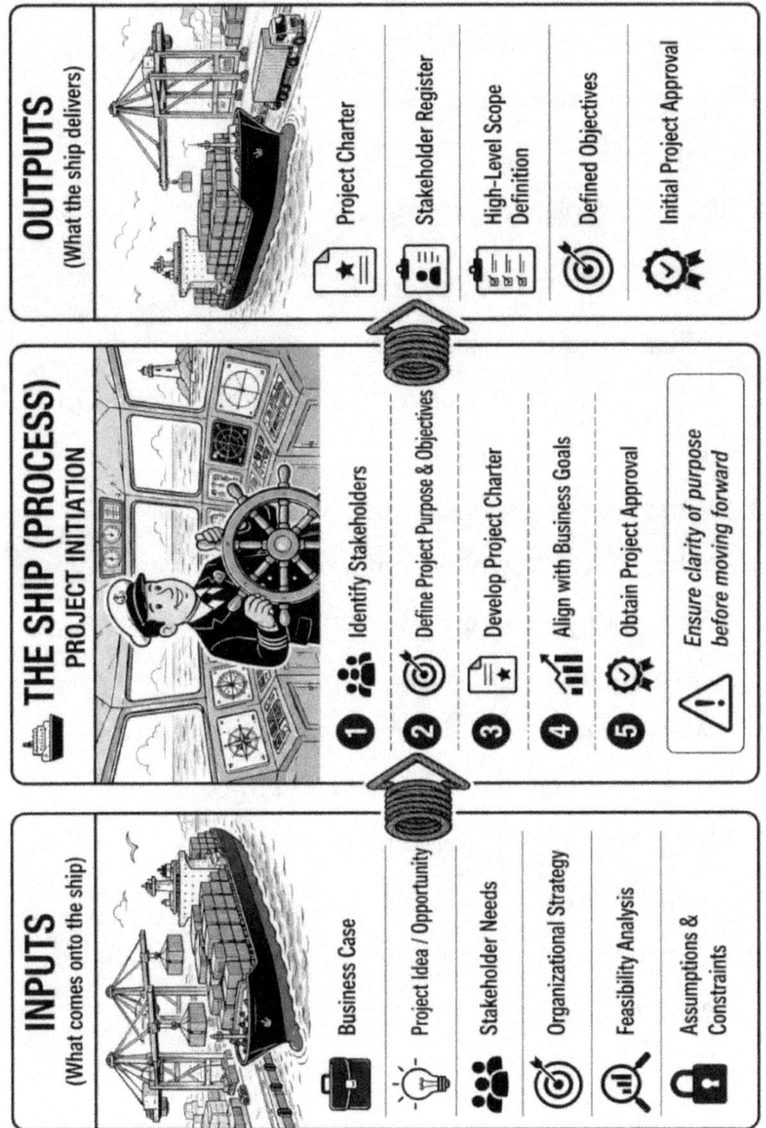

⚓ *Key Takeaways*

✓ Project management is both a discipline and a mindset

✓ Every project follows a lifecycle, even if informal

✓ The project manager guides direction, alignment, and outcomes

✓ Structure and planning increase the likelihood of success

End-of-Chapter Questions

1. What is project management?

2. Why is project management important in both formal and informal settings?

3. What are the responsibilities of a project manager?

4. What are the key phases of a project lifecycle?

5. How does project management apply to everyday tasks and responsibilities?

6. Why is structure important in managing a project?

7. How does planning contribute to project success?

8. What role does leadership play in project management?

9. How does project management improve decision-making?

10. Why is alignment among team members important in a project?

📓 *Captain's Log: Discussion Board*

Recall a time when you had to complete an important task at work, school, or in your personal life. What challenges did you face, and how did you overcome them? Reflect on how using project management methods might have enhanced the results.

Chapter 2: Scope Shores
(Project Initiation / Scope Planning)

⌖ *Learning Objectives*

By the end of this chapter, you should be able to:

- ✓ Define project scope and explain its importance
- ✓ Identify key components of a project scope statement
- ✓ Understand how scope influences project success
- ✓ Recognize the risks of unclear or poorly defined scope
- ✓ Explain what scope creep is and how to manage it

CHAPTER 2

Scope Shores

⚓ *Entering Scope Shores*

The river ahead looks calm, but appearances can be deceiving.

As the captain grips the wheel, a wide shoreline appears in the distance. It's not open water anymore. It's defined. Narrow. Controlled.

"Welcome to Scope Shores," the captain says.

The crew looks ahead. Some are excited. Others are unsure. "Out there," the captain continues, pointing behind them, "you can drift. You can explore. But here… you must decide."

A young crew member asks, "Decide what?"

The captain smiles slightly. "What we will do… and what we will not do."

The boat slows as it approaches the shoreline. Markers begin to appear in the water, boundaries, limits, and directions.

"If we don't define our path here," the captain says, "we'll run aground later."

Why Scope Matters

Every project begins with an idea or inspiration, but not all ideas have the potential to develop into successful projects. Several factors influence whether an idea can become a viable and impactful project. These factors include comprehensive planning, detailed requirements, resource access, and adaptability to obstacles. Although some ideas may appear promising initially, they require thorough assessment and proper implementation to become meaningful projects.

In many real-world situations, projects fail not because teams lack effort, but because they lack clarity. A team may begin work with enthusiasm, only to discover midway through that expectations are unclear or constantly changing. Without a clearly defined scope, team members may interpret the project differently, leading to misaligned efforts, duplicated work, and missed objectives. Over time, this confusion frustrates stakeholders and delays progress, ultimately putting the project's success at risk.

The fundamental reality is that if you don't take the time to explicitly outline the work involved, the project will likely take on a life of its own, often leading to unfavorable outcomes. A clearly defined scope establishes the limits and parameters of a project, ensuring that everyone is on the same page about its goals and deliverables. Without well-defined boundaries, what starts as a structured endeavor can easily devolve into a chaotic, unfocused effort, losing its intended purpose and direction.

What Is Project Scope?

The project scope is a detailed outline of the tasks and activities needed to create a specific product, service, or result.

It provides a framework that defines the work involved, including objectives, deliverables, and the overall vision of the project. By clearly stating what is included and what is not, the project scope helps ensure that all stakeholders have a shared understanding of the project's goals and expectations. This clarity supports effective resource management and sets the foundation for successful project execution.

It answers:

- What are we building?

- What are we delivering?

- What is included?

- What is excluded?

The Two Types of Scope (Critical Concept)

This is where people often get confused, so we'll keep it simple. One of the most important distinctions in project management is understanding the difference between product scope and project scope. While these concepts are closely related, they serve different purposes and must both be clearly defined to ensure project success. Product scope focuses on what is being created, while project scope focuses on the work needed to create it. Confusing these two can result in gaps in planning or incomplete deliverables, so it's essential for project managers to clearly define both at the start of the project.

1. Product Scope	**2. Project Scope**
What are you creating?	What it takes to create it?
Examples:	Examples:
A mobile app	Design
A website	Development
A coffee brand	Testing
A Classroom Project	Documentation

Scope Creep (The Hidden Danger)

Scope creep often starts with small, seemingly harmless changes. A stakeholder might request a minor adjustment, thinking it will improve the final result. Because the change seems minor, it's often approved without fully understanding its impact. But as more changes add up, the project gradually expands beyond its original scope. What began as a clear effort becomes harder to manage, putting pressure on the schedule, budget, and team. Without proper control, scope creep can quietly undermine even the best-planned projects.

Examples:

- "Can we just add one more feature?"

- "This should be quick…"

- "Let's improve this while we're here…"

What happens next:

- Timeline increases

- Costs increase

- Team stress increases

- Quality decreases

Captain's Rule: "If it's not in scope… It's not happening."

The Scope Foundation (What You Must Define)

Every project needs these four elements:

✓ **Objectives** - What are we trying to achieve?

✓ **Deliverables** - What will we produce?

✓ **Boundaries** - What is included/excluded?

✓ **Success Criteria** - How do we know we're done?

The Work Breakdown Structure (WBS)

Now we begin transforming ideas into structure. Breaking down a project into smaller (actionable) tasks is one of the most effective ways to handle complexity. Large projects can seem overwhelming when seen as a whole, but when divided into smaller, manageable sections, they become easier to plan, assign, and carry out. The Work Breakdown Structure (WBS) provides a structured way to organize this division, ensuring no major parts are missed. By clearly defining each level of work, project managers can improve accuracy in scheduling, cost estimation, and resource distribution.

A WBS divides a project into smaller parts. Think of it like this:

Project → Phases → Tasks → Subtasks (Actionable)

Why WBS Matters:

- Makes work manageable

- Helps estimate time and cost

- Prevents missing work

- Creates accountability

Figure 2.1 Example Work Breakdown Structure

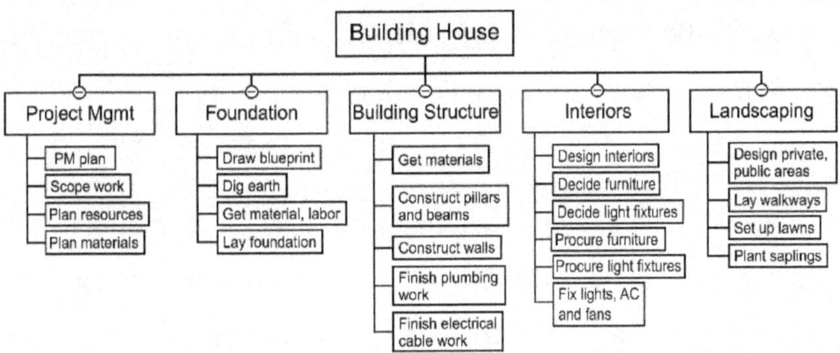

Break your tasks down into actionable items that feed your **Activity List.**

Real-World Example: Building a house

Imagine you're managing a project to build a house. At first, the idea seems simple: design a home, hire a builder, and start construction. However, without a clear scope, the project can quickly become complicated and hard to manage. The product scope here refers to the final house itself, including the number of bedrooms, kitchen size, living space layout, and overall design features. These elements define what is being created and what the finished product should look like.

The **project scope**, on the other hand, focuses on the work required to build the house. This includes activities such as hiring an architect, securing permits, preparing the land, laying the foundation, framing the structure, installing electrical and plumbing systems, and completing interior finishes. Each of these tasks must be planned, sequenced, and executed properly to ensure the home is completed successfully. Without clearly identifying this work upfront, it becomes difficult to estimate timelines, costs, and resource needs.

Now consider what happens when the scope is not clearly defined. Midway through construction, the homeowner decides to add an extra room, upgrade the kitchen, or install new features that were not part of the original plan. While these changes may seem reasonable, they introduce additional work, increase costs, and extend the timeline. This is a classic example of **scope creep**, where changes are made without proper planning or approval. Over time, these small additions can significantly affect the project's success.

By clearly defining both the product scope and project scope at the beginning, the project manager establishes boundaries and expectations for everyone involved. The team understands what needs to be built, what work is required, and what falls outside the agreed-upon scope. This clarity helps prevent confusion, reduces risk, and keeps the project on track. Just like navigating through Scope Shores, defining the path early ensures the journey ahead is controlled, intentional, and successful.

As projects become more complex, clearly defining the scope becomes even more essential. A well-defined scope not only sets expectations but also protects the project from unnecessary changes and confusion. By taking the time to fully understand and document what is included and what is not, project managers lay a strong foundation for planning, execution, and success. Going forward, this clarity will act as a guiding compass for every decision throughout the project lifecycle.

In the context of your Project Management Plan, this chapter marks the point where your project begins to take shape. The decisions you make about scope will influence every part of your plan moving forward, including scheduling, budgeting, and risk management. Taking the time to clearly define your scope now will make the remaining chapters more structured and easier to complete.

When starting your Project Management Plan, the first step is to clearly outline your project's scope. This serves as a foundation for making decisions about scheduling, budgeting, and resource allocation in later chapters. Defining a solid scope now helps avoid confusion in the future.

Reflection Questions

Recall a time when a task or project became more complex than expected. Was the scope clearly outlined at the start? What could have been done differently to avoid confusion or extra work?

Connecting to Your Project (Project 1)

At this point in your Project Management Plan, you are establishing the foundation of your project. The work you do in this section will influence everything that comes afterward. You will begin by clearly defining your project scope, including what is and is not part of it. This includes identifying your project's objectives, deliverables, boundaries, and success criteria. Taking the time to clearly define these elements now will avoid confusion and unnecessary revisions later.

Next, you will start breaking your project into smaller, manageable parts using a Work Breakdown Structure (WBS). This step helps you organize your work, making it easier to plan, schedule, and estimate costs in the following chapters. Your goal is to go from a broad idea to a clearly defined scope.

Full Steam Ahead - Process Port

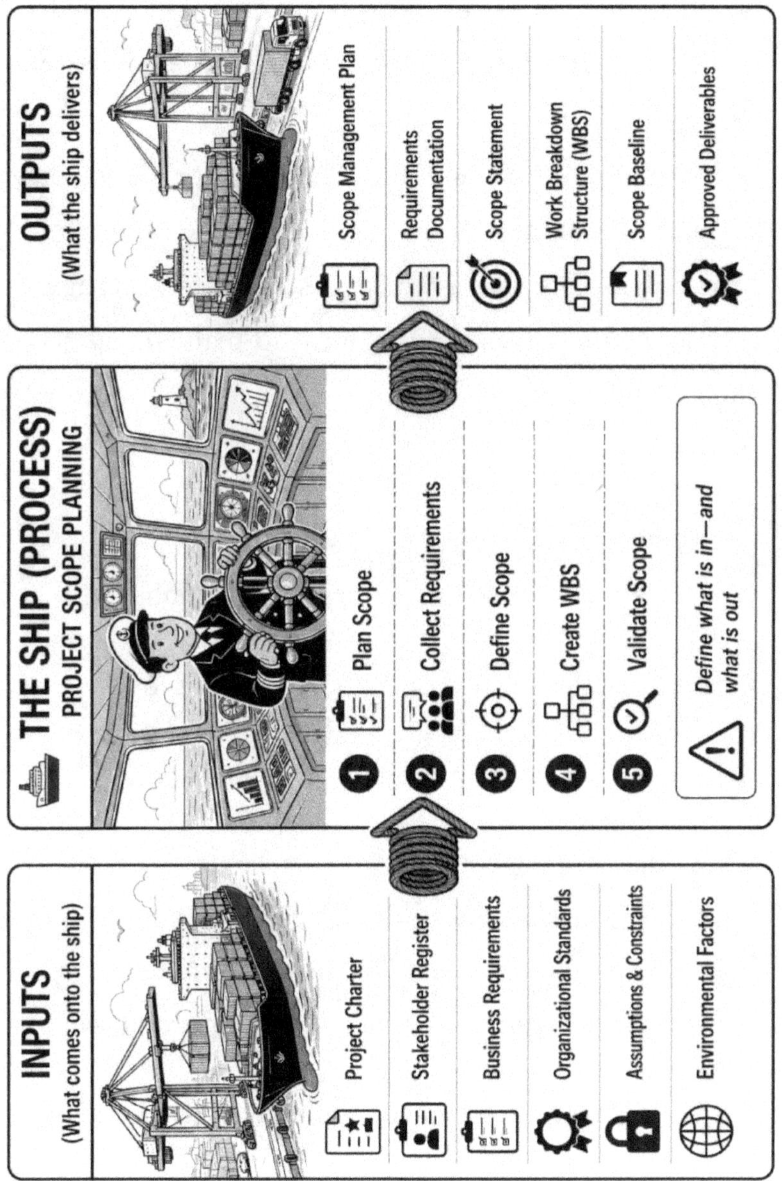

⚓ *Key Takeaways*

✓ Scope defines what is included and excluded in a project

✓ A clearly defined scope sets expectations and prevents confusion

✓ Scope is the foundation for planning, scheduling, and resource allocation

✓ Scope creep can derail a project if not properly managed

✓ Effective communication is critical to maintaining scope alignment

End-of-Chapter Questions

1. What is the project scope?
2. Why is defining scope important at the beginning of a project?
3. What key elements are included in a project scope statement?
4. How does scope influence project planning and execution?
5. What is scope creep?
6. What are common causes of scope creep?
7. How can scope creep negatively impact a project?
8. What strategies can be used to manage or prevent scope creep?
9. Why is stakeholder alignment important when defining scope?
10. How does a clearly defined scope contribute to project success?

📓 *Captain's Log: Discussion Board*

Reflect on a time when unclear or shifting expectations for a task or project caused challenges. How did this impact the outcome? Think about how clearly defining the scope from the start could have improved alignment, minimized confusion, and resulted in a better outcome.

Chapter 3 – Schedule Shoals
(Time / Schedule Planning)

🎯 *Learning Objectives*

By the end of this chapter, you should be able to:

- ✓ Understand the importance of project scheduling
- ✓ Identify the key components of a project schedule
- ✓ Explain how activities and dependencies are defined
- ✓ Recognize the role of sequencing and timelines in project success
- ✓ Understand how scheduling tools support project execution

CHAPTER 3

Schedule Shoals

⚓ *Entering Schedule Shoals*

As Captain Brian steers the *Deliverables* downriver, the waters begin to change. The wide, open river narrows, and jagged rocks—known as shoals—start to appear just beneath the surface. From a distance, the water looks calm, but hidden dangers threaten to slow the journey or damage the ship if not carefully navigated.

Without a clear path and precise timing, the boat could easily drift into trouble. Every turn must be calculated, every movement intentional. The crew must know not only where they are going, but *when* they need to arrive and what obstacles lie ahead.

In project management, this is the reality of scheduling. A project without a well-defined schedule may appear to be progressing, but beneath the surface, risks are forming. Delays, bottlenecks, and misaligned tasks can quickly throw the entire project off course. Just as navigating shoals requires foresight, planning, and constant awareness, managing time does as well.

What Is Project Scheduling?

Project scheduling is crucial for completing tasks efficiently and on time. By defining the timing and order of activities, it helps project managers allocate resources effectively. This organized method acts as a roadmap, guiding the project team through each phase.

While the project scope defines the specific deliverables and objectives, the schedule outlines the timeline for completing them. This includes setting deadlines for each task, establishing milestones to monitor progress, and allocating resources efficiently to keep the project on track. A well-organized schedule helps manage dependencies among tasks, allowing for smoother transitions and better coordination among team members, ultimately ensuring the project is finished within the desired timeframe.

A project schedule transforms a list of tasks into a timeline of execution. It answers critical questions such as:

- What needs to happen first?

- What can happen at the same time?

- What must be completed before something else can begin?

- How long will the entire project take?

Without a well-structured schedule, even clearly defined projects can face significant challenges in maintaining momentum. Teams risk starting their tasks too early, often before necessary resources or information are available. This can lead to wasted effort and potential misdirection.

On the other hand, starting work too late can lead to tight deadlines, increased stress, and lower-quality output. Also, doing tasks out of the intended order can cause confusion among team members, as they may have to wait for dependencies that haven't been addressed, leading to more delays and issues in the project timeline. Essentially, the lack of a detailed schedule can disrupt workflow, cause uncertainty, and ultimately hinder a project's overall success. Understanding what a schedule is only tells part of the story. Its true value lies in how it drives project success

Why Scheduling Matters

Time is often seen as one of the most limited and constrained resources in project management. Unlike financial resources or physical assets, once time is gone, it can't be recovered or replaced, creating a unique challenge for project leaders. Each delay in the project schedule causes a ripple effect, impacting not only the immediate task but also affecting other dependencies, team dynamics, and ultimately the delivery of the final product or service.

When a project schedule is unclear and poorly defined, teams tend to work reactively. This can cause a chaotic workflow, with work piling up in some phases while others face unnecessary downtime. Such an imbalance may lead to lower efficiency, increased frustration among team members, and a higher likelihood of mistakes as individuals rush to meet deadlines or manage competing priorities.

On the other hand, a well-organized and clearly outlined schedule serves as the backbone of any project. It provides the essential framework for project managers to establish clear expectations for all team members, ensuring everyone understands their responsibilities and timelines. This proactive strategy enables continuous progress monitoring and allows project leaders to spot potential delays early, addressing them before they become bigger problems.

A solid schedule enhances team confidence by providing a clear sense of direction and purpose. When every team member understands their tasks and deadlines, it fosters accountability and improves collaboration. This structured approach ultimately contributes to a more successful project outcome.

Understanding Task Dependencies

In any project, not all tasks can be executed simultaneously due to inherent relationships among them, known as dependencies. These dependencies dictate the order in which tasks must be completed, as some activities depend on the successful completion of others.

For instance, consider the construction of a house: before any painting can take place, the walls must first be constructed. This sequence ensures that the painting is not only effective but also protects the integrity of the work done on the walls. Similarly, in software development, testing cannot commence until the actual software has been fully developed. Testing before development would be futile, as there would be no functional product to evaluate. Understanding and managing these dependencies is crucial for effective project planning and execution, allowing teams to allocate resources and time efficiently while minimizing potential roadblocks.

Dependencies are essential in project management because they determine the proper order of tasks. Clearly identifying these dependencies helps teams focus on the right activities at the right time. This organized method prevents team members from jumping ahead to tasks that can't be completed until earlier steps are finished.

Understanding and managing dependencies can greatly improve workflow efficiency. Handling these dependencies helps teams reduce delays and rework. This proactive strategy ultimately supports completing projects on time.

There are four primary types of dependencies:

- **Finish-to-Start (FS):** A task must finish before the next one begins

- **Start-to-Start (SS):** Two tasks can begin at the same time

- **Finish-to-Finish (FF):** Two tasks must finish at the same time

- **Start-to-Finish (SF):** A rare relationship where one task must start before another finishes

Understanding the links between different parts of a project is essential for effective management. By understanding these connections, project managers can develop schedules that accurately reflect timelines and resource availability. This insight ultimately results in more efficient project execution and improved outcomes.

From WBS to Schedule

A Work Breakdown Structure shows what work needs to be done, but it does not specify when that work will happen. Scheduling involves arranging the listed tasks in a logical order over time. Without this step, a project is just a bunch of tasks instead of a coordinated plan.

In Chapter 2, we discussed the Work Breakdown Structure (WBS) as a tool to break the project into smaller, manageable parts. This method allowed us to pinpoint specific tasks and deliverables. As a result, the overall project became easier to understand and manage effectively.

Once we have outlined the components, the next important task is to organize them in a logical sequence. By doing so, we can ensure that each task is completed in the correct order, taking into account any dependencies and timelines. This careful sequencing is essential for maintaining project momentum and achieving timely completion.

Each work package from the WBS becomes a **scheduled activity**. The project manager must:

1. Identify the order of tasks

2. Estimate how long each task will take

3. Assign dependencies

4. Place tasks on a timeline

This process converts a static work list into a flexible plan ready for execution.

Critical Path (The River's Main Channel)

Every project schedule features a defined sequence of tasks that is vital for estimating the minimum completion time. This key sequence of activities is known as the **critical path**. Understanding the critical path helps project managers optimize timelines and ensure efficient resource allocation.

The critical path is defined by the longest sequence of dependent activities, meaning that each task along this path depends on the successful and timely completion of the previous tasks. If any of these critical tasks are delayed, the entire project schedule is at risk, causing a ripple effect that could postpone all subsequent activities.

To visualize the critical path, think of it as the main channel of a river. While the river might have smaller tributaries and side streams that offer limited flow, it is the main channel that determines how quickly a boat can reach its destination. Any obstacle along this central route can greatly delay progress and prevent the project from meeting its goals.

In contrast, tasks outside the critical path may have some flexibility, often called "float." This means these non-critical tasks can be delayed slightly without impacting the overall project delivery. However, it is essential to remember that tasks on the critical path have no float; they are time-sensitive and must be completed on schedule to keep the project on track. Managing these critical tasks effectively is key to successful project management and on-time delivery.

Float (Slack) – Room to Breathe

Not every task in a project is equally urgent. Some tasks have built-in flexibility, allowing them to be delayed without affecting the overall project timeline. This flexibility is called **float** or **slack**.

Float offers the project team some breathing room, enabling small adjustments without major disruptions. Nevertheless, overreliance on float can be risky, as accumulated delays might turn previously flexible tasks into critical ones. Knowing how to manage float helps project managers prioritize work and allocate resources efficiently.

Real-World Example: Building a House - Project Timeline

Imagine you're in charge of managing the construction of a house, a project that demands careful planning and execution to ensure everything is completed successfully. The project scope has already been clearly defined, providing you with a blueprint of what needs to be built. Your next crucial task is to decide the order and timing of each construction step, which is vital for maintaining efficiency and meeting deadlines.

The construction process starts with laying the foundation, a vital first step that creates the base for the entire structure. This foundation must be carefully laid and fully cured before any framing work begins. Once the foundation is stable, you can start the framing process, where the house's skeletal structure is built. This includes walls, beams, and roof trusses that give the house its shape and support.

After finishing the framing, the next step is installing essential systems like electrical wiring and plumbing. These installations require careful coordination because they must be integrated into the walls and other structures before the walls are closed up. It's crucial that these systems are completed and inspected to meet building codes before drywall can be installed.

After finishing the electrical and plumbing work, the next step is to install drywall, which turns the raw framed structure into enclosed rooms. Once the drywall is up, the walls can be painted and finished with trim, fixtures, and other decorative elements that improve the home's appearance and usefulness.

It's important to realize that any delay in laying the foundation will trigger a chain reaction affecting all subsequent tasks. This delay in the foundation directly influences the overall project schedule and is considered part of what project managers call the critical path. In contrast, tasks like landscaping can be scheduled after the house is finished and can be delayed without impacting the project's overall completion date. These tasks are known as having float, providing some flexibility in scheduling.

Throughout the construction process, as the project manager, you must consistently monitor the overall schedule. This requires regularly checking the progress of each task against the planned timeline. If any task falls behind schedule, you may need to make adjustments. This could involve reallocating resources, rescheduling other tasks, or even bringing in additional labor to keep the project on track.

As the project moves forward, delays may threaten the overall schedule, requiring the project manager to take corrective action. Two common methods used to regain lost time are **crashing** and **fast tracking**. Crashing means adding additional resources to a task, like hiring more workers for framing or extending work hours to accelerate progress. Although this can reduce the time needed for critical tasks, it usually raises costs. Fast tracking, on the other hand, involves executing tasks simultaneously that were initially scheduled one after the other.

For instance, beginning interior work before completing all exterior construction can save time. However, this approach also carries risks, as overlapping tasks may require rework if initial activities are not completed properly. Both strategies demand careful consideration because they involve balancing time, cost, and risk. They should be used judiciously to ensure the project stays on schedule and maintains quality.

Effective scheduling turns a simple list of tasks into a well-coordinated plan. This method ensures each phase of the project flows smoothly into the next. Ultimately, it plays a key role in keeping the project's timeline and efficiency on track.

Common Scheduling Mistakes

Many projects struggle not because of poor scope, but because of weak scheduling practices.

Common mistakes include:

- Underestimating how long tasks will take

- Ignoring dependencies between tasks

- Failing to identify the critical path

- Not updating the schedule as the project progresses

- Overloading team members without considering capacity

Avoiding these mistakes requires careful planning and continuous monitoring.

Connecting to Your Project (Project 1)

At this point in your Project Management Plan, your project should already have a clearly defined scope. With this scope in place, your next task is to organize it into a realistic and actionable schedule. This step is vital because an effective schedule will guide the project from beginning to end and help ensure a successful completion.

You will start by identifying all the major tasks involved in the project. It's crucial to determine the order of these tasks because it will affect how the project progresses over time. Also, estimating how long each task will take is important for creating an accurate timeline that reflects the project's needs and limitations.

As you create your schedule, pay close attention to task dependencies. Understanding how tasks interact with and depend on each other will help you manage the workflow more effectively. Additionally, identifying your project's critical path is essential, as it shows the sequence of tasks that directly affect the project's completion time.

The schedule you develop will serve as the main timeline for your project, providing a framework that shapes every decision going forward. Keep in mind that elements like resources, costs, and risks are all affected by this schedule, so thoughtful planning at this stage will be beneficial in the long term.

Reflection Questions

Reflect on a time when a project or assignment took longer than you expected. Were tasks completed out of order? Were dependencies overlooked? Was the time required underestimated? If you were to plan that project today, what would you do differently?

Closing Thought

A project without a schedule is like a ship without a navigation plan. It may move forward, but it lacks direction and control. Careful planning of the sequence and timing of your work creates a clear path through the uncertainties ahead. As you progress, your schedule will serve as your guide, helping you navigate challenges and stay on course toward successful completion.

⬭ Captain's Reminder

The schedule is not only about time but also about timing. Performing the right work at an improper time can still cause failure.

Full Steam Ahead - Process Port

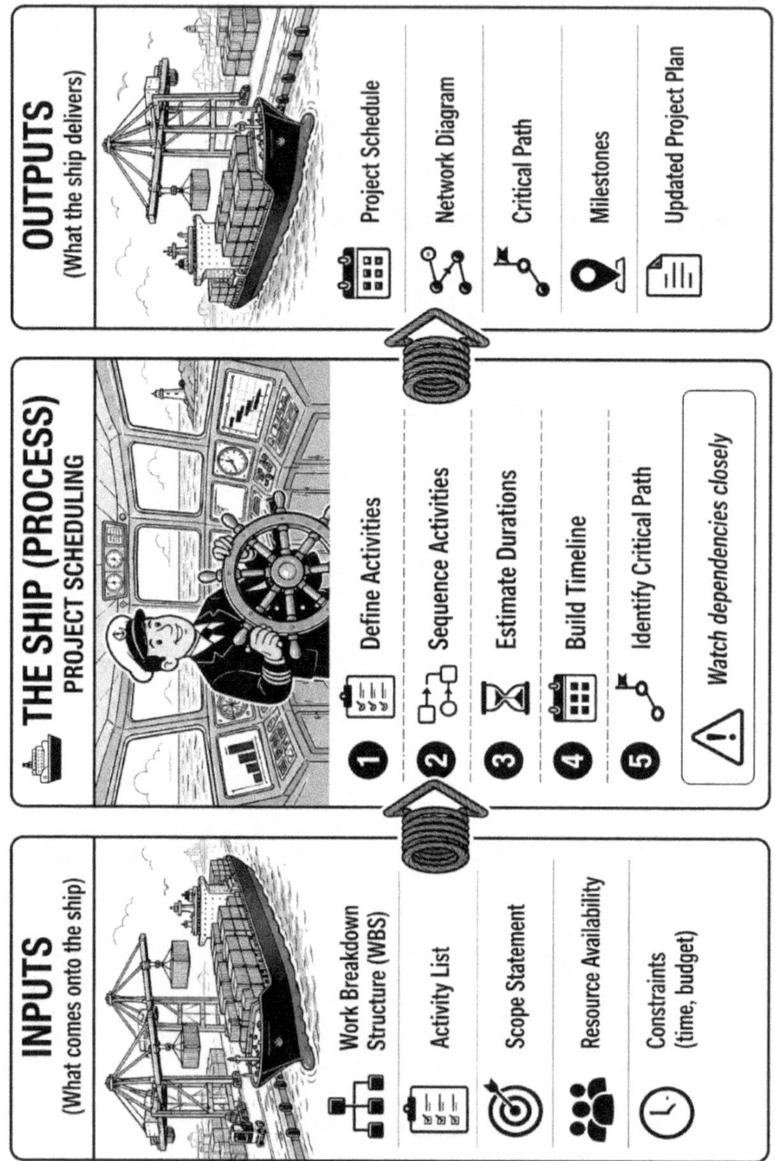

⚓ *Key Takeaways*

- ✓ A schedule translates scope into actionable timelines
- ✓ Activities must be clearly defined and properly sequenced
- ✓ Dependencies determine the order in which work is performed
- ✓ A well-structured schedule improves coordination and efficiency

End-of-Chapter Questions

1. What is a project schedule?
2. Why is scheduling important in project management?
3. What are project activities, and how are they defined?
4. What are dependencies in a project schedule?
5. What are the different types of dependencies?
6. How does sequencing activities impact project timelines?
7. What is a milestone in a project schedule?
8. How can poor scheduling affect project outcomes?
9. What tools are commonly used to manage project schedules?
10. How does a project schedule support team coordination and execution?

📖 *Captain's Log: Discussion Board*

Recall a time when inadequate planning or poor timing influenced the result of a task or project. What were the issues, and how did they affect the final outcome? Consider how establishing a detailed schedule with specific activities, dependencies, and deadlines might have enhanced the situation and contributed to a more favorable result.

Chapter 4 – Cost & Quality Coves

(Cost & Quality Management)

🎯 *Learning Objectives*

By the end of this chapter, you should be able to:

- ✓ Understand the role of cost management in project success
- ✓ Identify key components of a project budget
- ✓ Explain how cost estimation supports planning and decision-making
- ✓ Understand the importance of quality management in delivering value
- ✓ Recognize the relationship between cost, quality, and project outcomes

CHAPTER 4

Cost & Quality Coves

⚓ *Entering Cost & Quality Coves*

As the ship, Deliverables, continues its journey along the winding river, the water begins to widen, transforming into a serene stretch lined with small, inviting coves that cradle the shoreline. The tranquil scene offers the crew an opportunity to pause, gather their thoughts, assess their current position, and prepare strategically for the upcoming challenges of the voyage.

Captain Brian, observing the gentle ripples on the surface of the water, raises his hand to signal the crew to gradually reduce the vessel's speed. "Welcome to Cost & Quality Coves," he remarks solemnly, the weight of the moment evident in his voice. "This is a critical juncture where many voyages either find their way back on track or quietly unravel."

As the crew absorbs the captain's words, a sense of confusion flickers across their faces. One crew member, still staring at the placid waters, questions, "But Captain, the river seems so calm; what threats could possibly lie ahead?"

Captain Brian nods thoughtfully, understanding their concerns. "That's precisely the problem," he replies, his tone firm. "The danger here is not immediately apparent. It lurks just beneath the surface, revealing itself gradually through overspending on resources, cutting corners in our efforts, or hastily rushing through critical tasks."

He gestures toward the picturesque shoreline dotted with lush greenery and rocky outcrops. "If we invest too much without careful planning, we risk running out of vital resources before our journey comes to its conclusion. Conversely, if we rush through our work in an attempt to save time, we may find ourselves facing the bitter consequences of compromised quality that often require significant rework down the line."

The crew understands the captain's message, shifting from confusion to clarity. "This is where we must make critical decisions," the captain emphasizes, his voice steady and commanding. "Here, we determine the resources, time, money, and effort needed, and how well we must perform to ensure success." The crew feels the weight of responsibility, ready to navigate difficult decisions ahead.

Understanding Project Cost

At its core, cost management answers a simple question: how much will this take? Every project requires the allocation and management of different resources, each of which involves a financial expense. These resources include labor, such as team members' and contractors' work, materials used in construction or manufacturing, equipment needed for operations, and external services, such as consulting or specialized labor. Each part of the project contributes significantly to the overall budget, making accurate cost management essential.

Effective project cost management involves a systematic approach to estimating, budgeting, and controlling costs throughout the project's lifecycle. This process starts with a detailed cost estimate that predicts the expenses associated with each project activity. This initial estimate serves as the basis for a comprehensive budget that details how funds will be distributed across the project's phases and components.

Once the budget is established, ongoing monitoring and controlling of costs become essential. This involves regularly comparing actual expenditures against the budgeted amounts and analyzing variances to identify areas that may require corrective action. Without diligent cost planning and oversight, projects can quickly spiral out of control, leading to budget overruns. These situations can place considerable pressure on stakeholders such as investors, clients, and team members, thereby reducing the project's overall value and threatening its success.

It is important to understand that a project's cost extends beyond just financial expenses. It includes how effectively resources are used to reach the desired results. High efficiency means that goals are achieved without waste, maximizing the return on investment for everyone involved. By paying attention to both the financial side of cost management and the proper use of resources, project managers can ensure the project is completed successfully within budget and provides maximum value.

Cost Estimation

Cost estimation is crucial in project management, acting as a key step in accurately predicting the expected expenses for each task or activity outlined in the project plan. This detailed process starts with a comprehensive activity list carefully developed during earlier planning phases. By examining this list, project managers can identify the costs involved, making sure that every element is considered and that the overall budget is both practical and effective in guiding the project's financial plan.

For each activity in the project, several key factors must be analyzed to arrive at an accurate cost estimate:

✓ **Labor Costs**: This includes all expenses related to the project workforce. It covers salaries or hourly wages, benefits, and other employee costs. Detailed estimates include determining staff requirements, their roles, duration of involvement, and any anticipated overtime.

✓ **Material Costs**: This encompasses all physical items necessary for executing the project activities, including raw materials and finished goods. Cost estimation requires identifying these items, researching their current market prices, and accounting for transportation or storage costs associated with them.

✓ **Equipment Costs**: These costs include all tools and equipment needed for the project. Estimating these costs involves deciding whether to buy, lease, or rent the equipment, and considering any maintenance or operating expenses associated with the machinery.

✓ **External Costs**: These costs cover outsourcing or engaging third-party vendors or specialized services outside the internal team. This can include subcontracting tasks, hiring consultants, or buying services that improve project results.

Accurate cost estimation goes beyond simple calculations; it requires careful planning and thoughtful decision-making. It is crucial to examine every component thoroughly before making projections. This approach helps ensure more reliable and informed financial forecasts.

Underestimating costs can significantly affect the project's budget and overall success, potentially causing financial overruns and resource shortages. Therefore, a careful approach that combines data analysis with experienced insight is crucial for creating accurate cost estimates. On the other hand, overestimating may make the project seem less feasible.

The Project Budget (Cost Baseline)

Once all individual project costs have been estimated, they are aggregated to formulate the project budget, commonly referred to as the **Cost Baseline**. This cost baseline represents the total anticipated expenditure required to successfully complete the project. It is more than just a figure; it serves as a crucial reference point for monitoring and evaluating financial performance throughout the entire project lifecycle.

By establishing a baseline, project managers can monitor actual costs against the planned budget, helping track financial health and make informed decisions to keep the project on track. Regularly comparing actual expenses to the cost baseline enables the identification of variances, prompts timely corrective measures as needed, and supports overall effective financial management.

Every project, no matter its size or complexity, faces uncertainties that can affect its success. To handle these uncertainties effectively, project managers usually include a **Range of Magnitude (ROM)** or a contingency buffer in their plans. This contingency buffer serves as a financial cushion to cover unexpected variables, risks, and potential changes that may occur during the project's lifecycle.

Including a contingency buffer is essential because unexpected events, from small changes in scope to major disruptions, can quickly delay the project and go over the budget. Even minor surprises can add up, leading to big costs if not planned for. By proactively setting aside a buffer for these uncertainties, project managers can improve their project's resilience, reduce the chance of budget overruns, and help ensure a smoother process toward successful completion.

Cost and the Triple Constraint

Cost should never be seen as an isolated factor. Instead, it is closely connected to both the project's scope and timeline. When a project's scope expands, whether through new features, requirements, or deliverables, this typically results in higher overall costs. The reason is simple: more extensive projects usually require more resources, such as additional labor, materials, or technology.

Similarly, if the project schedule is shortened, costs are likely to increase as well. This often happens because a compressed timeline usually requires allocating more resources in less time. For example, project managers might need to hire extra staff or pay overtime to meet tighter deadlines, which can significantly raise the overall budget.

Efforts to reduce costs can significantly affect a project's scope or schedule. Cutting the budget might mean trimming certain features or sacrificing quality. These changes could also cause delays as the project team adapts to them.

Project managers are essential for handling the complexities of project execution, as they must skillfully manage various interconnected trade-offs throughout the project's lifecycle. Each financial decision can significantly impact the project's timeline, scope, and quality. Consequently, it is crucial for project managers to understand how these factors relate to one another. Recognizing the complex dependencies between time constraints, budgets, and quality standards is key to guiding the project successfully and achieving all objectives in harmony.

- ✓ Increasing scope → increases cost
- ✓ Shortening schedule → increases cost (more resources)
- ✓ Reducing cost → may reduce scope or extend schedule

Understanding Quality in Projects

At its core, quality answers another simple question: how well must this be done? Quality in project management goes beyond simply striving for perfection. It encompasses the critical ability to understand and fulfill clearly defined requirements and expectations of stakeholders. This process involves not only following established standards and specifications but also making sure that the final deliverables meet the project's intended goals and objectives.

Delivering quality means ensuring that the final results align with the project scope. It involves meeting stakeholder expectations as well as the initial objectives. The ultimate aim is to achieve the intended impact and functionality specified in the project plan.

Effective quality management requires a systematic approach to meet established standards and customer expectations. It involves setting quality standards, planning, and implementing continuous quality control measures. Additionally, ongoing improvement efforts are essential to enhance overall quality and performance.

Effective quality management fundamentally involves setting clear quality goals and establishing processes that help organizations reliably produce excellent results. This can include training employees on best practices, adopting quality assurance measures, and using tools like statistical process control to track performance.

Additionally, effective quality management involves regularly reviewing and improving processes based on feedback from customers and stakeholders. Promoting a culture of quality within the organization ensures that each team member understands their role in achieving overall quality goals, encouraging accountability and collaboration.

Ultimately, the goal of effective quality management is not only to meet regulatory requirements but also to improve customer satisfaction, reduce costs related to defects and rework, and gain a competitive edge in the marketplace. It requires a clear understanding of the needs of all parties involved, proactive communication, and ongoing assessment throughout the project lifecycle. By focusing on these key areas, project managers can ensure the output meets or exceeds expectations, ultimately leading to successful project outcomes.

A project can be deemed to exhibit high quality when it successfully aligns with the following criteria:

Stakeholder Expectations: The project should not only identify stakeholders' expectations but also actively involve them by understanding their needs, preferences, and concerns. This ensures their objectives are reflected in the project's results.

Requirements Fulfillment: Every project is based on a set of requirements that specify the essential features, functions, and constraints. A high-quality project effectively fulfills these requirements, ensuring all deliverables are produced as specified.

Performance as Intended: Quality in project management goes beyond merely adhering to technical specifications; it is primarily about how well the project deliverables meet their intended purpose and function as expected, ensuring stakeholders receive the anticipated benefits. The final product or service must operate properly and deliver the expected advantages without significant issues.

Quality is intentional, not accidental, and requires careful planning from the beginning of a project. By setting quality criteria, measurable standards, and benchmarks early on, it becomes clear what success looks like. Quality should be regularly monitored and assessed during the execution phase to allow for timely adjustments and improvements, ensuring alignment with goals and stakeholder expectations. Incorporating quality at every stage of project management increases the likelihood of delivering successful outcomes that satisfy all involved parties.

The Cost of Poor Quality

In many organizations, teams often fall into the trap of trying to save both time and money by taking shortcuts in their processes. This approach might seem like an efficient solution in the short run because it can lead to faster project completion and lower immediate costs. However, this strategy often causes more serious problems later, including defects, rework, and missed deadlines.

Cutting corners often reduces the quality of deliverables, leading to unhappy stakeholders. This decrease in quality not only damages the organization's reputation but also can cause long-term issues. In the end, the costs of fixing errors, handling complaints, and missing business opportunities can greatly surpass any short-term savings.

Maintaining high standards of quality is essential to avoid pitfalls and foster a culture of excellence within teams. By investing time and resources in quality, organizations encourage continuous improvement among their members. This focus on quality ultimately helps companies avoid costly consequences that can arise from hasty decisions in the name of efficiency.

Poor quality in deliverables can lead to a variety of significant consequences, including:

Rework: This involves revisiting tasks that were not completed correctly initially, which often demands extra resources and time. The requirement to redo work can delay project schedules and shift focus away from other important aspects activities.

Delays in Delivery: When quality issues occur, the project timeline may be extended. These delays can impact not only the current project but also subsequent ones that depend on its timely completion, potentially causing a cascading effect on the overall workflow.

Increased Costs: The financial implications of poor quality are significant. Besides the direct costs of redoing work, there are indirect costs, such as potential penalties, overtime, or hiring extra staff to meet deadlines. This can strain budgets and affect overall profitability.

Loss of Stakeholder Trust: Persistent quality issues can erode stakeholders' confidence in a project or organization. Once trust is broken, it can be hard to rebuild, which may lead to strained relationships and potential loss of future business. In many instances, fixing errors later costs much more than doing it correctly from the beginning. This underscores the importance of prioritizing quality early on in a project.

By allocating resources and effort to establish high standards and thorough practices from the outset, organizations can ensure smoother processes and superior results. Investing in quality helps minimize mistakes and enhances efficiency, ultimately saving time and money. A proactive approach to quality fosters a culture of excellence, which boosts productivity and improves customer satisfaction.

Balancing Cost and Quality

A natural tension exists between cost and quality in any project or production process. Recognizing this balance is essential for success. When organizations underfund their projects, they risk lowering the quality of their products or services. This can lead to issues such as using inferior materials, employing less-skilled labor, or neglecting details, which may cause customer dissatisfaction and harm the brand's reputation over time.

Exceeding the necessary budget can result in wasted resources. For example, intentionally adding unrequested features, functionality, or "extras" to a deliverable beyond the agreed-upon scope, often to impress stakeholders, known as **Gold Plating** and **Scope Creep**, can harm the project's overall Return On Investment (ROI).

ROI is a financial metric that measures the profitability or efficiency of an investment. It is determined by comparing the investment's gain or loss to its initial cost. Essentially, ROI expresses this as a percentage, showing the profit or loss made. This helps investors and businesses evaluate the success of their investments and make informed decisions about resource allocation to maximize returns.

The pressure to accelerate work to meet tight deadlines can negatively affect quality. Rushing increases the risk of mistakes and missing details, resulting in costly rework or repairs that may outweigh the initial time savings. Meanwhile, over-engineering can raise project costs by adding features or capabilities that do not meet user needs or project goals, creating complexity without real benefits.

The goal is to improve quality without compromising cost. The real challenge is to find the right balance between these two factors. Achieving this balance ensures sustainable and efficient outcomes that align with project goals and user expectations.

Common Cost & Quality Mistakes

Common project challenges come from poor oversight of costs and quality. This mismanagement can cause budget overruns, poor deliverables, and ultimately project failure. When teams fail to monitor spending and uphold quality standards, they risk harming the project's overall success and stakeholder satisfaction. It's essential for project leaders to adopt strong strategies that carefully track financial resources and consistently maintain quality standards throughout the project's lifecycle.

Several common pitfalls can contribute to these struggles:

1. **Underestimating Costs**: Many project managers overlook the importance of thorough cost analyses, which can lead to budget overruns. It's crucial to consider all aspects of a project, such as materials, labor, and unexpected expenses. Proper planning helps ensure that projects stay on track financially.

2. **Failing to Include Contingency Buffers**: A common mistake in project management is not allocating funds for contingencies. These financial buffers are essential for

handling unexpected challenges that may occur during the project. Without them, any changes in scope can disrupt progress and put pressure on resources.

3. **Ignoring Quality Requirements**: Ignoring quality requirements might seem advantageous initially, but it typically leads to increased costs later from rework, defects, or unhappy customers. Consistently following quality standards is essential throughout the project.

4. **Cutting Corners to Save Money**: Cutting corners on quality might seem like an easy way to save time and resources initially. However, it can lead to higher costs in the long run due to rework and potential customer dissatisfaction. Setting and following clear quality standards is crucial for the success of any project.

5. **Not Tracking Costs During Execution**: Projects need continuous cost monitoring to keep spending within the budget. Without regular tracking and reports, costs can quickly get out of control, making it hard to resolve issues as they happen.

To effectively avoid these common mistakes, thorough planning, ongoing monitoring, and strict discipline throughout the project's execution are essential. Using these practices helps ensure that projects are finished on time, within budget, and meet the desired quality standards.

Real-World Example: Building a House Budget & Quality Decisions

Imagine you're managing the construction of a house, with the scope and schedule already set. To ensure the project's success, you need to create a detailed budget that covers all anticipated costs. At the same time, it's crucial to establish clear quality standards to meet your expectations. By balancing the budget and quality, you help ensure a positive outcome for the project.

Each part of the house incurs a cost. Materials such as lumber, concrete, and roofing need to be purchased. Skilled workers are required for framing, electrical work, plumbing, and finishing. Equipment might be needed for excavation and building. As these costs are estimated, they are combined to create the project budget.

However, decisions must be made about quality. For example, you might choose between standard materials and premium materials for flooring, countertops, or fixtures. Higher-quality materials often cost more but tend to last longer and require less maintenance over time. Lower-cost materials may reduce the initial budget but could lead to repairs or replacements later.

Now consider what happens if costs exceed the budget. You might need to make trade-offs, such as reducing certain features, selecting cheaper materials, or extending the schedule to distribute expenses. Each of these decisions impacts the project's final outcome. On the other hand, trying to save money by cutting corners can result in poor quality. For example, rushing installation or using substandard materials may cause structural problems or system failures. Fixing these issues later can be more costly than doing the work correctly from the start.

As the project manager, your role is to carefully balance these decisions. You need to ensure the project remains within budget while still delivering a home that meets quality standards. This requires ongoing monitoring, thoughtful decision-making, and a clear understanding of priorities.

Connecting to Your Project (Project 1)

At this stage of your Project Management Plan, you will delve into the critical task of assigning costs to each of your project activities, which lays the groundwork for developing a comprehensive cost baseline. This baseline serves as a financial reference point throughout the project's lifecycle, helping you track expenses and ensure that you remain within budget.

In addition to financial planning, you will define your quality measurement criteria. This involves thoroughly identifying the specific requirements your deliverables must meet to satisfy stakeholder expectations. It is essential to outline the success metrics that will be used to evaluate the effectiveness of your project's outcomes.

The processes outlined in this chapter are crucial. They will affect your project's financial stability and significantly impact its overall effectiveness and success. Thoughtful planning at this stage can ensure sustainable outcomes and increase the chances of achieving or surpassing your project goals.

Reflection Questions

Reflect on a time when a task was completed quickly or at a lower cost, only to later require extra effort to fix issues. What caused the issue? Was quality sacrificed to save time or cost? What would you do differently now? This highlights the importance of balancing efficiency and quality in our work.

Closing Thought

A project that strictly follows its budget but fails to meet quality expectations cannot be considered a true success. Conversely, delivering high-quality results with substantial budget overruns can threaten the project's long-term viability. True success in project management depends on balancing budget adherence with maintaining or surpassing quality standards.

As you navigate the complexities of your project journey, it's important to remember that every decision incurs a cost, and each one has its own set of consequences. Whether these decisions involve resource allocation, timeline adjustments, or quality control, managing them carefully and strategically distinguishes an average project from an outstanding one.

This attentive management not only increases the chances of project success but also promotes a culture of accountability and excellence within your team. Balancing financial responsibility with a dedication to quality will ultimately lead to more sustainable results and greater stakeholder satisfaction.

Full Steam Ahead - Process Port

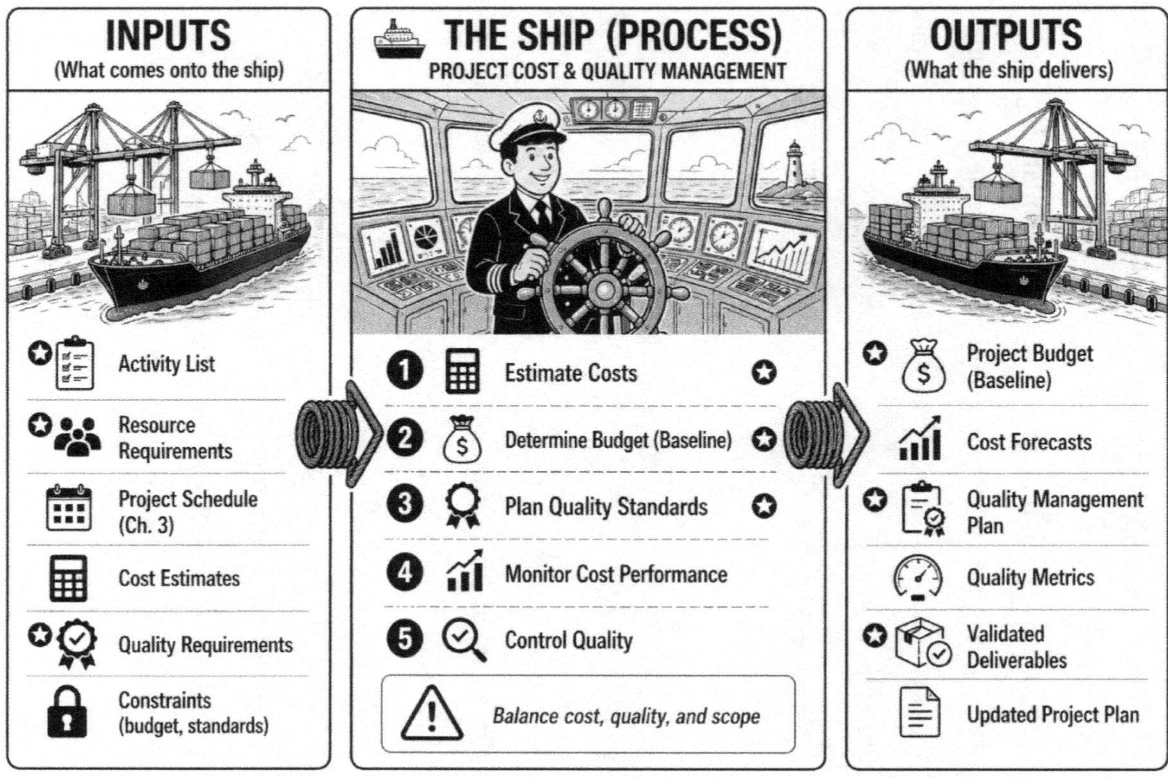

⚓ *Key Takeaways*

✓ Cost management ensures the project stays within approved financial limits

✓ Accurate estimation is critical for realistic planning

✓ Budgets provide a financial roadmap for project execution

✓ Quality management ensures deliverables meet defined standards

✓ Balancing cost and quality is essential for overall project success

End-of-Chapter Questions

1. What is cost management in a project?

2. Why is budgeting important for project success?

3. What are the key components of a project budget?

4. What is cost estimation, and why is it important?

5. What factors can influence project costs?

6. What is quality management in project management?

7. Why is quality important in delivering project outcomes?

8. How can poor quality impact a project?

9. What's the relationship between cost and quality in a project?

10. How can a project manager balance cost constraints while maintaining quality?

Captain's Log: Discussion Board

Reflect on a situation in which cost or quality influenced the outcome of a task or project. Did you cut corners to save time or money, or was additional effort necessary to enhance quality? Reflect on how balancing cost and quality could have led to a better outcome and what decisions could have been made differently.

Chapter 5 – Resource River

(Resources & Communication)

🎯 *Learning Objectives*

By the end of this chapter, you should be able to:

- ✓ Understand the importance of resource management in projects
- ✓ Identify different types of project resources (human, material, and equipment)
- ✓ Explain how roles and responsibilities are defined within a project team
- ✓ Understand the role of communication in managing resources effectively
- ✓ Recognize how proper resource allocation impacts project success

CHAPTER 5

Resource River

⚓ *Entering Resource River*

As the *Deliverables* ship leaves The Coves, the river widens again. The current remains steady, but onboard activity picks up. Crew members move purposefully, each handling a different part of the journey.

Captain Brian stands at the helm, observing. "This is Resource River," he says. "From here on out, the journey depends less on the river… and more on the crew."

A new crew member looks around. "But we've already planned everything," they say. "Shouldn't it just run smoothly now?"

The captain smiles. "Plans don't execute themselves," he replies. "People do."

He gestures across the ship. "Every role matters. Every task depends on someone doing their part and doing it at the right time."

The crew begins to understand. "And if we don't communicate," the captain adds, "even the best plan will fall apart."

Understanding Project Resources

At its core, resource management centers on a critical question: who and what do we need to achieve our project objectives? Successful project completion depends not only on organizing tasks and setting timelines but also on the strategic allocation of the right people, tools, and materials to execute the required work. These essential components are classified as project resources, which must be meticulously planned, assigned, and managed throughout the project's lifecycle.

Resources can be grouped into three primary categories:

Human Resources: This encompasses the individuals who contribute to the project's success, including team members who carry out the work, managers who oversee progress and provide guidance, and stakeholders who have a vested interest in the project's outcomes. Understanding each person's unique skills, strengths, and availability is crucial for maximizing efficiency and collaboration.

Physical Resources: This category includes all tangible assets required for project execution, such as equipment, materials, facilities, and other physical tools. Proper management of these resources ensures they are available when needed and maintained in good working order, preventing delays and interruptions in the project timeline.

Technical Resources: These include the software, systems, and tools used for project planning, monitoring, and execution. To use technical resources effectively, it's important to choose platforms and technologies that fit the project's needs, train team members to use them, and integrate them smoothly into their workflows.

Each type of resource plays a distinct and vital role in the overall project framework. Without the appropriate resources in place, even the most meticulously planned project is likely to face significant obstacles that hinder progress and potentially jeopardize success. Therefore, thorough resource identification, allocation, and ongoing management are essential practices for any project manager aiming to lead their team toward achieving their goals efficiently.

Roles and Responsibilities

A successful project team is more than just a collection of individuals; it requires a well-defined structure with clear roles for each member. To be effective, every team member must understand their responsibilities and how they support the team's overall goals. Strong communication and collaboration are essential for reaching project objectives. Therefore, it is important that each member has a thorough understanding of these key aspects:

Individual Responsibilities: Each member should understand their specific responsibilities and the extent of their work. This clarity promotes effective focus of efforts and resources, ensuring everyone is aware of their expectations.

Timeline for Deliverables: Team members should have a clear understanding of their task deadlines. Knowing when their contributions are required within the project timeline enables better planning and prioritization, minimizing the risk of delays.

Interconnectivity of Tasks: Team members need to understand how their work fits with and supports others' work. Recognizing these links encourages collaboration, allowing team members to see the broader context and value of their roles in achieving the project's overall objectives.

When roles are not clearly defined, a cloud of confusion can quickly engulf the team. This lack of clarity can lead to numerous problems: tasks might be duplicated, deadlines might be missed, or assignments might be executed incorrectly due to misunderstandings.

Defining clear roles helps reduce risks and encourages accountability within the team. Assigning specific owners to each part of the project ensures expectations are communicated clearly from the beginning. This groundwork boosts team efficiency and effectiveness, increasing the likelihood of project success.

Common Resource Management Mistakes

Projects frequently encounter numerous significant challenges when resource management lacks careful planning and accuracy. Poor resource management can extend project timelines, resulting in project overruns. It can also cause unforeseen budget overruns, putting financial strain on the project and restricting future prospects. As these issues accumulate, team morale may decline, fostering frustration and lowering motivation among team members.

Some common mistakes that project managers and teams might make include:

Overloading Individuals: Assigning too many tasks to a single person can lead to burnout and reduced productivity. It's vital to recognize each team member's capacity and distribute the workload evenly to maintain efficiency and morale.

Ambiguous Roles and Responsibilities: Failing to clearly assign responsibilities can lead to confusion, redundant work, and missed deadlines. Defining clear roles promotes accountability and helps create a more organized workflow.

Neglecting Resource Availability: Failing to evaluate the availability of resources, such as personnel, equipment, or budget, can significantly delay the project timeline. Regular assessment and planning for these resources can help avoid avoidable setbacks.

Underestimating Team Needs: Neglecting the importance of team interactions and communication can result in misunderstandings and conflicts among members. Promoting open dialogue and creating a collaborative atmosphere are crucial for effective teamwork.

Resistance to Adaptation: Failing to adjust resources as the project develops is a major mistake. Projects frequently undergo shifts in scope, priorities, and obstacles that necessitate reassessing resource deployment. Staying adaptable and responsive to these changes can significantly improve project success.

Proactive planning is crucial to avoid common pitfalls in project management. Maintaining awareness of team needs and being adaptable throughout the project lifecycle can greatly enhance the chances of success. By focusing on these areas, teams can effectively achieve their project goals.

The Importance of Communication

Human Resources in a project consists of the individuals responsible for executing specific roles.

135

Communication plays a crucial role in maintaining alignment with organizational goals by keeping all stakeholders informed. Effective communication addresses the key question of how to stay connected and aware of the project's progress and challenges.

Effective communication is crucial among team members, stakeholders, and leadership in a constantly evolving project environment. Timely and accurate information sharing is necessary, as different phases of the project often involve various components. Clear communication ensures that all parts operate seamlessly together.

Effective communication plays a crucial role in ensuring that:

✓ Everyone involved understands the overall project plan, including roles, responsibilities, and timelines.

✓ Potential issues are identified and addressed early, preventing escalation and ensuring that obstacles are proactively managed.

✓ Decision-making processes are expedited and efficient, with all relevant information considered to facilitate swift and informed choices.

✓ Teams remain aligned and focused on their shared goals, fostering collaboration and unity of purpose.

Without effective communication mechanisms, highly skilled teams may still struggle with collaboration. Disconnections can cause misunderstandings or delays, ultimately affecting project success.

Effective communication strategies must be prioritized to keep all parties engaged. This ensures that everyone stays informed throughout the project lifecycle. By doing so, we can promote a cohesive and productive working environment.

Common Communication Challenges

Communication failures are a major cause of project failures, making it essential to address them for successful outcomes. They often arise from different factors that disrupt effective teamwork and clarity. Below are some typical causes of poor communication:

Lack of Clear Communication Channels: When teams lack defined methods or channels for sharing information, confusion often occurs. This might involve not having dedicated tools for messaging, video calls, or project management, which can result in messages being lost or ignored.

Information Overload: Conversely, an excess of communication can overwhelm team members, causing important details to be overlooked. When teams are bombarded with emails, updates, and discussions, distinguishing urgent matters from routine information becomes challenging, leading to decreased productivity and engagement.

Lack of Visibility: Conversely, poor communication can leave team members feeling disconnected from the project's progress. When updates are not regularly shared, individuals may struggle to understand the full project status, leading to misalignment and delays in task completion.

Misinterpretation of Messages: Communication involves more than just transmitting information; it requires the recipient to understand it correctly. Misunderstandings may arise from unclear language, cultural differences, or tone, leading to actions that diverge from the project's objectives.

Failure to Communicate Changes: Changes to project scope, timelines, or team roles are inevitable during a project. However, if these adjustments are not communicated clearly and promptly, they can cause uncertainty, disrupt workflows, and result in resistance from team members.

Communication challenges can cause serious problems, such as confusion among team members and missed deadlines due to misaligned expectations. This often leads to increased frustration and harms team morale. To ensure project success, teams must recognize these issues early and adopt effective communication strategies proactively.

Communication Is Not Just Talking

Effective communication extends beyond speech; it involves a complex interaction among parties. This process involves not only transmitting and receiving messages but also ensuring that everyone understands one another. Ultimately, successful communication aims to establish mutual understanding among all participants.

A successful message depends on clear communication to make sure the recipient fully understands it. Essential elements such as clarity, context, and relevance are vital to conveying the right meaning. Effective messaging helps build stronger connections and reduces the risk of misunderstandings. This necessitates several key components:

Active Listening: This goes beyond just hearing what someone is saying. It requires giving the speaker full attention, engaging with their message, and replying thoughtfully. Active listeners often use verbal acknowledgments and non-verbal signals to demonstrate their engagement.

Clear Messaging: Clarity in the message is crucial for effective communication. This means using straightforward language, structuring thoughts logically, and avoiding ambiguity. The sender should tailor the message to the audience's level of understanding, ensuring it resonates and is easy to digest.

Feedback and Confirmation: After delivering a message, it's important to request feedback. This might include asking the recipient to paraphrase their understanding or encouraging questions to clear up any confusion. Confirmation helps prevent miscommunication and allows for adjustments if needed.

Effective communication doesn't occur by chance; it demands deliberate effort and planning. By staying mindful and proactive, people can significantly elevate the quality of their interactions. Using strategic methods promotes stronger connections and improves overall communication.

Real-World Example: Building a House Team & Communication

Imagine you are managing the construction of a house, and your scope, schedule, and budget have already been defined. Now, the project's success depends on the people involved and how well they work together. The project includes various teams such as architects, contractors, electricians, plumbers, and inspectors, each with designated roles that require careful coordination. The framing team needs to complete their work before the electricians and plumbers begin, and inspectors must assess progress at key milestones.

Unclear role definitions can lead to confusion. For instance, when two teams assume the other is responsible for a task, it may result in no work being done. Additionally, if several teams try to handle the same task, it wastes resources and hinders progress.

Communication becomes equally important. The project manager must ensure that updates are shared regularly, changes are communicated clearly, and any issues are addressed quickly. If the electrician is not informed that framing has been delayed, they may arrive on-site unprepared, causing scheduling conflicts and wasted time.

In this environment, success depends not only on the plan but also on how effectively people execute it and communicate with each other. A well-coordinated team can overcome challenges, while a poorly coordinated team can struggle even with a strong plan.

Connecting to Your Project (Project 1)

At this stage of your Project Management Plan, it is crucial to begin identifying the key personnel and resources required to successfully complete your project. This involves a thorough analysis of the project requirements and clear documentation of how to meet them.

Clearly define each team member's role in the project by detailing their responsibilities and key deliverables. Include roles such as project manager, team leads, and support staff, along with their specific duties. Additionally, specify the authority and decision-making power assigned to each person. This clear delineation promotes accountability and helps everyone understand their part in ensuring the project's success.

For each major task in your project, create a detailed list of required resources, such as personnel, budgets, equipment, software, and other materials needed. Breaking down resource allocation this way helps identify potential gaps and ensures all requirements are met effectively and efficiently.

Plan how communication will be handled during the project. Schedule regular check-ins, updates, and meetings to ensure continuous dialogue among team members and stakeholders. Specify communication channels, such as email, project management tools, or face-to-face meetings, and ensure everyone knows when and how to share updates. Setting clear rules for communication frequency and formats helps reduce misunderstandings.

Your main goal with these elements is to guarantee that all parts of your project are adequately supported and that the team shares a unified goal. Creating a comprehensive resource and communication plan will help your project operate smoothly, greatly lowering the chances of misunderstandings and delays that could disrupt timelines and impact overall success.

Reflection Questions

Think about a time when a group project or team effort did not go as planned. Were the roles clearly defined? Was communication consistent and effective? What actions could have been done differently to improve coordination?

Closing Thought

A project is only as strong as the people who bring it to life. Plans provide direction, but the team drives execution. By explicitly defining roles and ensuring effective communication, you create an environment where success is possible. As you continue your journey, remember that managing people is not just part of the project; it is the heart of it.

Full Steam Ahead - Process Port

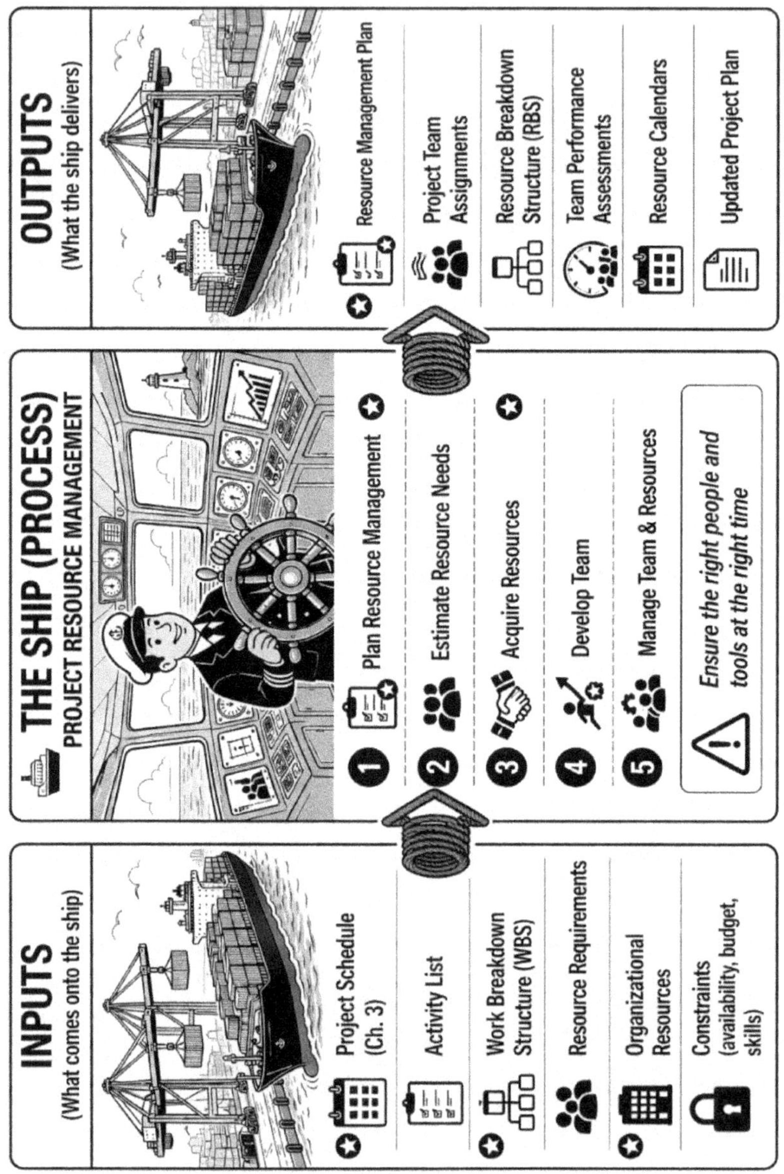

⚓ *Key Takeaways*

- ✓ Resources include people, materials, tools, and equipment
- ✓ Clearly defined roles improve accountability and efficiency
- ✓ Effective communication keeps the team aligned and informed
- ✓ Resource allocation must be balanced to avoid overload or delays
- ✓ Strong team coordination drives project performance and success

End-of-Chapter Questions

1. What is resource management in project management?
2. What are the different types of resources used in a project?
3. Why is it important to define roles and responsibilities within a project team?
4. What is the purpose of a responsibility assignment matrix (RAM) or RACI?
5. How does communication support effective resource management?
6. What challenges can arise from poor resource allocation?
7. How can over-allocation of resources impact a project?
8. What strategies can be used to manage team communication effectively?

9. How does teamwork contribute to project success?

10. Why is coordination among team members critical in a project?

📓 *Captain's Log: Discussion Board*

Recall a time when collaborating on a task or project did not go smoothly. What issues arose regarding roles, communication, or workload? Consider how clearer responsibilities and improved communication might have enhanced teamwork and resulted in a better outcome.

Chapter 6 – Risky Rapids

(Risk Management)

⌖ Learning Objectives

By the end of this chapter, you will be able to:

✓ Understand what risk is and how it impacts projects

✓ Differentiate between positive and negative risks

✓ Identify common sources of risk in projects

✓ Perform basic risk identification and assessment

✓ Understand risk response strategies

✓ Recognize the importance of proactive risk management

✓ Apply risk planning to your Project Management Plan

CHAPTER 6

Risky Rapids

⚓ *Entering Risky Rapids*

As the *Deliverables* continues its journey, the calm waters begin to shift. The steady current gives way to turbulence, and the sound of rushing water grows louder ahead.

Captain Brian grips the wheel firmly. "Prepare yourselves," he calls out. "We're entering Risky Rapids."

The crew looks ahead and sees whitewater crashing against jagged rocks. The once predictable river is now chaotic and uncertain.

"Can we avoid this?" one crew member asks.

The captain shakes his head. "Not entirely. Every journey has risks. The key isn't avoiding them, it's preparing for them."

The boat surges forward, and the crew braces themselves.

"Some of these currents can push us off course," the captain continues. "Others might actually speed us up, but only if we know how to handle them."

The crew tightens their grip.

"Stay alert," Captain Brian says. "This is where planning meets reality."

Understanding Risk in Projects

At its core, risk management addresses a fundamental question: what potential events or conditions could arise and affect our project's success? A risk is any uncertain event or condition that, if it occurs, could significantly influence the project's objectives. These influences can be categorized into two main types: negative impacts, known as threats, and positive impacts, referred to as opportunities.

Risk is often perceived primarily in terms of negative outcomes, which can lead to a narrow understanding of its true nature. In reality, risk also includes potential benefits that should not be overlooked. For example, while implementing new technology may involve uncertainty, it can ultimately improve efficiency and reduce costs over time.

To manage risks effectively, it is essential to recognize that uncertainty is inherent in every project, regardless of its nature or scale. Acknowledging this fact is crucial because disregarding risks does not eliminate them; instead, it leaves the project vulnerable and unprepared to respond to unexpected challenges or seize valuable opportunities. By adopting a proactive approach to risk management, project teams can better navigate uncertainty, formulate strategic responses, and improve overall project outcomes.

Types of Risk: Threats and Opportunities

Risks in project management can be classified into two primary categories:

Threats: Potential events or conditions that may adversely affect the project's objectives. Threats can take many forms, including delays in the project timeline, significant cost increases, or the failure of critical components. For instance, a threat could arise from unforeseen circumstances such as supply chain disruptions, unexpected regulatory changes, or lapses in team performance. It is essential for project managers to identify these threats early and develop mitigation strategies to minimize their impact on the project's success.

Opportunities: Favorable events or conditions that could lead to positive outcomes for the project. These might include opportunities for cost savings through more efficient processes, the possibility of completing the project ahead of schedule, or enhancements that improve the overall quality of the deliverables. Recognizing these opportunities is crucial, as they can significantly contribute to the project's success and overall value to stakeholders.

Effective project managers adopt a balanced approach to risk management by planning for both threats and opportunities. While it is vital to implement strategies to mitigate potential threats, it is equally important to actively seek out and capitalize on opportunities that may arise throughout the project lifecycle. By cultivating a proactive mindset, project managers can both protect the project from possible risks and leverage opportunities that foster success and innovation.

Risk Identification

Effective risk management begins with a systematic identification of potential risks that could impact a project. This proactive approach is essential for reducing negative consequences on project outcomes. Recognizing risks early allows teams to implement strategies to mitigate them before they materialize.

Risks can originate from a variety of sources, each presenting unique challenges. Some key categories include:

Technical Challenges: The challenges we face often stem from the technology's complexity. This includes problems such as software bugs leading to unexpected issues, system incompatibilities that disrupt smooth integration, or design limitations that restrict functionality. Overcoming these obstacles typically requires ongoing review and adjustments throughout the project to stay responsive to new complexities and modify our strategies as needed.

Resource Limitations: The availability of critical resources, such as skilled personnel, suitable equipment, and high-quality materials, is vital to a project's success. When any of these resources are scarce or limited, it can lead to delays and negatively affect the quality of deliverables. For example, inadequate staffing may increase the workload for current team members, and the absence of proper tools or materials can slow production. These constraints can ultimately block a project's progress and undermine its initial goals.

Budget Constraints: Financial constraints can significantly limit a project's scope, making it harder to hire qualified professionals or purchase necessary materials. Continuous monitoring of budget allocations against actual expenses is essential, as careful tracking helps ensure the project's long-term viability and success. Regular evaluations can detect potential financial problems early, enabling timely adjustments to keep the project on course.

Schedule Pressures: When faced with tight deadlines, the pressure to deliver quickly can become overwhelming, often leading to rushed work that sacrifices quality and effectiveness. To combat this, it is essential to periodically assess project timelines and adjust plans as needed. This proactive approach allows for the incorporation of unexpected delays, ensuring that final outcomes meet the desired standards rather than falling short due to rushed efforts. Regular evaluations help balance efficiency and quality, leading to more successful project completions.

External Factors: These factors are beyond the organization's direct control, including unpredictable weather that can impact operations and changes in regulations that might introduce new compliance standards. Additionally, fluctuations in market demand affect sales and inventory. By monitoring these external trends and developments, organizations can better anticipate potential challenges, adjust their strategies to reduce negative effects, and capitalize on emerging opportunities.

Risk Identification isn't just a one-time task; it's an ongoing, evolving process that must be embedded into every stage of project management. As projects progress, new risks may emerge at any time due to changing circumstances or unexpected events. It is important to establish continuous risk assessment and management methods throughout the project to detect and address potential threats promptly. This cyclical approach helps keep the project stable and increases the likelihood of successfully reaching objectives.

Risk Assessment (Likelihood & Impact)

Once the various risks have been identified, it becomes imperative to conduct a comprehensive evaluation to gain a deep understanding of their potential impacts on the project. This evaluation should consider not only the likelihood of each risk occurring but also the magnitude of its potential consequences, enabling the project team to prioritize their responses effectively and develop strategies to mitigate adverse effects.

Risk assessment essentially seeks to answer two fundamental questions:

What is the likelihood of this risk occurring?

This involves analyzing historical data, industry trends, and project-specific factors that could influence the likelihood of the risk materializing. Combining quantitative methods, such as statistical analysis, with qualitative assessments can provide a well-rounded perspective on likelihood.

What would be the impact if this risk occurred?

This question examines the consequences if the risk materializes, assessing how it could affect project timelines, costs, quality, and overall success. Impact analysis may involve scenarios to estimate the financial implications, resource strain, or reputational damage that could arise from each identified risk.

When managing risks, it is crucial to focus on those with high probability and impact, addressing them immediately to prevent substantial consequences for the organization or project. Conversely, lower-level risks, which present smaller threats or are less likely to occur, can usually be observed over time. While they may need careful monitoring to prevent escalation, they do not require urgent intervention. By clearly differentiating these risk categories, organizations can better allocate resources and formulate suitable response plans.

By carefully evaluating both the probability and consequences of each risk, project managers can effectively determine which risks need more focus and resources. This helps teams focus on the most critical risks that could threaten project goals, enabling them to develop appropriate mitigation measures and boost overall project resilience.

Risk Response Strategies

Once risks have been identified and thoroughly assessed, the next step is to determine the appropriate responses to these risks. This step is crucial to risk management and can significantly influence the success of a project or initiative. For potential threats, several common strategies can be employed, each serving a specific purpose in addressing the identified risks:

Avoid: This strategy completely removes the risk by changing the plan or approach. This could involve adjusting project goals, schedules, or methods to eliminate risk factors. For instance, if a project faces a high failure risk due to strict deadlines, extending the deadline or modifying the scope can help avoid the risk entirely.

Mitigate: When it is not possible to completely eliminate risks, mitigation strategies can be used to reduce either the likelihood of the risk occurring or its potential impact. This might include enhancing processes, adding safety measures, or using technology to decrease exposure. For example, if there is a risk of equipment failure during a crucial project phase, routine maintenance and inspections can help reduce that risk.

Transfer: This method involves transferring the risk to a third party, relieving the risk owner of the burden. It is typically accomplished through contracts, warranties, or insurance policies. For instance, a company might buy insurance to protect against losses from natural disasters, thus shifting the risk to the insurer.

Accept: Sometimes, even when a risk is identified, it may be considered acceptable depending on the potential impact, likelihood, or the resources needed for mitigation. In such cases, developing a response plan to be implemented if the risk happens is crucial. This approach usually involves monitoring the risk and collecting data to ensure a quick and effective response if it occurs.

When it comes to seizing opportunities, there are several strategic approaches one can take:

Exploit: This strategy emphasizes proactive steps to fully capitalize on the opportunity. It includes allocating resources, defining clear goals, and outlining specific actions to seize the moment and maximize benefits. A well-organized plan is essential to ensure the opportunity is not overlooked.

Enhance: By enhancing an opportunity, the aim is to increase both its chances of happening and its potential benefits. This can be achieved by investing time in research, building skills, networking, or creating favorable conditions. The intention is to proactively cultivate an environment that boosts the likelihood of the opportunity occurring and enhances its positive outcomes.

Share: This strategy highlights the importance of collaboration and partnerships. Working together with others allows you to capitalize on the opportunity more effectively. Sharing resources, knowledge, and networks can result in greater collective benefits than acting alone. This cooperative approach also creates new opportunities for exploration and innovation.

Accept: This approach focuses on being ready to take advantage of opportunities as they arise, instead of actively seeking them out. It involves being alert to opportunities and ready to act quickly. Successful implementation depends on adopting a mindset that prioritizes flexibility and adaptability, enabling you to respond effectively when an opportunity arises.

By understanding and applying these strategies, individuals and organizations can better navigate their landscape of opportunities, make more informed decisions, and remain proactive and responsive. The appropriate response depends on the nature of the risk and the project's goals. Not every risk requires action, but all must be understood.

In summary, selecting an appropriate response strategy involves carefully evaluating the specific risks, considering the situation's context, and assessing available resources for risk management. Each approach requires careful thought to manage risks effectively and ensure project objectives are met.

Proactive vs. Reactive Risk Management

A major difference between successful and struggling projects is how they handle risk.

Reactive teams often wait and see, letting problems develop before acting. By the time they respond, issues have typically caused delays, increased costs, or disruptions to progress. This slow reaction can lead to a chain of complications and lower team morale. Conversely, proactive teams focus on risk management, spotting potential problems early and addressing them before they become serious.

Proactive teams excel at identifying potential risks early. By anticipating challenges, they can develop strategic responses in advance. This approach enables them to respond quickly and effectively, reducing the negative impact of unexpected issues.

Effective risk management is not just about predicting the future with complete accuracy. Instead, it focuses on equipping teams with the tools and strategies to handle any uncertainties that may arise. By doing so, organizations can better prepare for potential challenges.

Common Risk Management Mistakes

Projects often face major difficulties if risks are not accurately identified, evaluated, and controlled. Lack of proper risk management can lead to unexpected problems that delay schedules, increase costs, and threaten the project's overall success.

Common mistakes include:

- Ignoring risks until they become problems

- Failing to identify risks early in the project

- Underestimating the likelihood or impact of risks

- Not developing response strategies

- Failing to monitor risks throughout the project

Avoiding these mistakes requires awareness, careful planning, and continuous evaluation to track progress and adjust accordingly. Staying alert, developing a strategic approach, and regularly reviewing results can greatly lower the chance of errors.

Real-World Example: Building a House and Managing Risk

Imagine you're managing the construction of a house with a fixed scope, schedule, budget, and resources. Even with a well-laid plan, unexpected challenges and uncertainties can occur during the project. It's essential to stay flexible and proactive in tackling these issues as they come up.

One potential risk is the weather. Heavy rain could delay foundation work, pushing back all subsequent activities. Another risk is supply chain issues, where critical materials such as lumber or fixtures are delayed. There may also be labor-related risks, such as a contractor becoming unavailable at a key stage of the project.

At the same time, opportunities could emerge. For instance, good weather might enable completing work sooner than planned. A supplier may provide discounted materials, lowering total expenses. Recognizing and managing these positive risks effectively can enhance project results.

As the project manager, you must identify these risks early and plan accordingly. For weather-related risks, you might build contingency time into your schedule. For supply risks, you might secure backup vendors. For labor risks, you might ensure that additional resources are available if needed.

Neglecting to plan for uncertainties can cause minor problems to escalate, potentially disrupting the whole project. Implementing effective risk management strategies enables you to address challenges proactively. This approach helps maintain the project's direction and supports consistent progress.

Connecting to Your Project (Project 1)

At this point in your Project Management Plan, it is crucial to begin identifying and evaluating potential risks that could significantly affect different parts of your project. A thorough risk analysis involves several key components:

Begin by identifying the key risks that could impact your project's scope, timeline, budget, and quality. Think about technical issues, resource constraints, regulatory updates, stakeholder involvement, and market trends. Collaborating with your team and stakeholders can help uncover a variety of potential risks.

For each identified risk, evaluate its likelihood and potential impact on the project if it occurs. Use either qualitative or quantitative methods to analyze these aspects. Developing a risk matrix can be especially useful for visualizing each risk's probability and severity, helping you prioritize them effectively.

Create detailed response plans for the most significant risks, especially those with high probability and impact. Explore different approaches like risk avoidance, mitigation, transfer, or acceptance. Clearly document these strategies, including specific steps, responsible parties, and necessary resources for execution.

Keep in mind that the goal isn't to eliminate all uncertainty from your project, but to be sufficiently prepared for it. A comprehensive and well-organized risk management plan will enable you to respond quickly and effectively to challenges, helping to keep your project on schedule and aligned with its goals. By actively managing risks, you improve your project's resilience and increase its chances of success.

Reflection Questions

Think about a time when an unexpected event affected a project, assignment, or plan. Was the risk identified beforehand? How did the situation affect the outcome? What could have been done to better prepare for it?

Closing Thought

Every project faces uncertainty. Some challenges will test your plans, while others might open up unforeseen opportunities. Success often depends on how well you prepare. By spotting risks early and preparing responses, you can navigate uncertainty confidently. Keep in mind that risk isn't something to fear, but something to manage.

Full Steam Ahead - Process Port

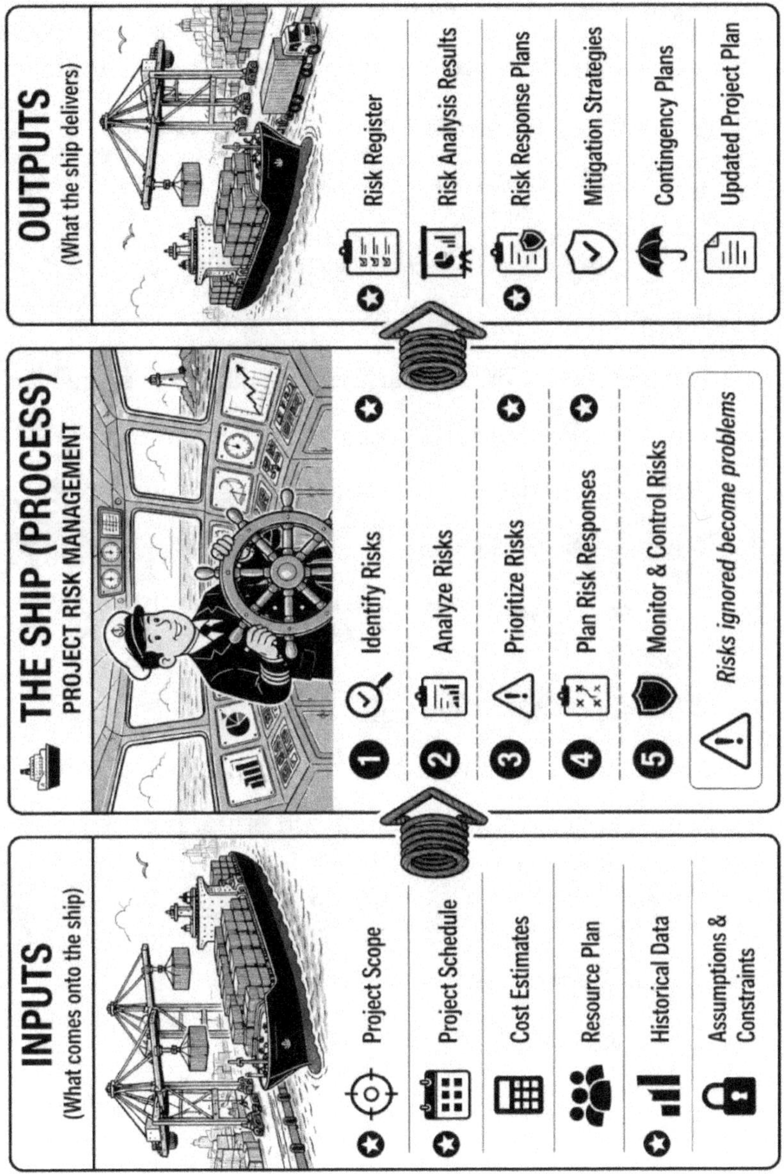

⚓ *Key Takeaways*

✓ Risk is any uncertain event that can impact a project

✓ Risks can be negative (threats) or positive (opportunities)

✓ Early identification of risks improves preparedness

✓ Risk assessment considers both likelihood and impact

End-of-Chapter Questions

1. What is risk in project management?

2. What is the difference between a risk and an issue?

3. What are the two main types of risks in a project?

4. Why is it important to identify risks early in a project?

5. What is a risk register?

6. How are risks assessed in terms of probability and impact?

7. What are common strategies for responding to risks?

8. How can risk management improve project outcomes?

9. What happens if risks are ignored or not properly managed?

10. How does risk management support decision-making in a project?

📖 *Captain's Log: Discussion Board*

Recall a moment when an unforeseen issue disrupted a task or project. Consider how you responded and how it affected the final result. Reflect on how early risk identification and proactive planning might have altered the situation and led to a better outcome.

Chapter 7 – Procurement Point
(Procurement Planning)

🎯 *Learning Objectives*

By the end of this chapter, you should be able to:

- ✓ Understand the purpose of procurement in project management
- ✓ Identify when and why external vendors are needed
- ✓ Explain the basic procurement process
- ✓ Recognize different types of contracts used in projects
- ✓ Understand the importance of managing vendor relationships

CHAPTER 7

Procurement Point

⚓ *Arriving at Procurement Point*

As the Deliverables continues its journey, the river narrows again, and a busy trading post appears along the shoreline. Boats are docked, supplies are loaded, and crews are negotiating with merchants.

Captain Brian slows the vessel. "We've arrived at Procurement Point," he says.

The crew looks around, noticing that not everything needed for the journey is aboard the ship. "Can't we just use what we already have?" one crew member asks.

The captain shakes his head. "Not always. Some parts of the journey require resources we don't have on hand."

He gestures toward the dock. "Sometimes we need to bring in outside help, including materials, tools, or expertise."

The crew observes another ship loading supplies. "But be cautious," the captain advises. "Relying on others means you can't fully control your success."

The crew begins to understand. "This is where we decide," the captain says, "what we do ourselves… and what we trust others to deliver."

Understanding Procurement

Procurement fundamentally asks: Which resources or services do we need to acquire externally to achieve and improve our project objectives? This process includes assessing our project needs, exploring the best marketplace options, and securing the essential tools, materials, and expertise to advance our initiatives. Effective procurement management helps align external offerings with our strategic goals, enabling the successful realization of our project objectives.

Procurement includes obtaining goods, services, or resources from outside the project team, which is vital for the project's success. While many tasks can be managed internally, there are numerous situations where bringing in external expertise, specialized materials, or additional support is essential to tackle challenges and meet particular project needs.

Key aspects of procurement may include but are not limited to:

Hiring Contractors or Consultants: In many projects, specialized skills or knowledge are required that the internal team cannot provide. Hiring external contractors or consultants enables access to industry specialists who offer valuable insights, skills, and experience, thereby improving the quality and execution of the project.

Purchasing Materials or Equipment: Some projects need special materials or equipment that might be difficult or expensive to make internally. Procurement helps by acquiring these essential items, making sure the project has the necessary tools and resources when needed.

Utilizing Third-Party Software or Services: In the fast-changing world of technology, projects often gain from using third-party software solutions or services that provide advanced features or increased efficiency. Procurement enables the selection and acquisition of these resources, helping streamline project workflows and boost overall productivity.

Effective procurement practices allow projects to tap into specialized skills and essential resources that may not be available within the internal team. This strategic approach enhances the project's overall capabilities and fosters innovation. As a result, it significantly contributes to achieving successful outcomes.

Make-or-Buy Decisions

A key early decision in procurement is whether to execute a task internally or outsource it. This fundamental choice asks: should we produce the goods or services ourselves, or is it better to buy them from the outside? Several important factors are crucial in this decision:

Cost Analysis: Conducting a comprehensive assessment of the financial impact of completing the work in-house versus contracting an external supplier is crucial. This evaluation should consider direct costs, such as labor and materials, as well as indirect expenses, including overhead and potential downtime.

Availability of Internal Expertise: It's crucial to evaluate if the organization has the right skills, knowledge, and resources to handle the work internally. If there is a deficiency in expertise, whether in quantity or quality, outsourcing may be necessary.

Time Constraints: Timelines can greatly affect decision-making. If a project faces tight deadlines that current internal resources can't meet, outsourcing might provide a faster alternative. External vendors often have more resources and specialized expertise, which can help accelerate project completion.

Quality Requirements: The target quality level of the final product influences whether to produce internally or hire external vendors. If the in-house team cannot reliably achieve high standards, outsourcing to specialized providers who can deliver better results may be a wise choice.

Risk Considerations: Outsourcing carries specific risks, including dependence on third-party vendors, potential quality problems, and supply chain interruptions. Therefore, it is crucial to assess the risks of both in-house production and external sourcing to identify which aligns best with the company's risk appetite and strategic goals.

Outsourcing tasks can save time, access specialized skills, and reduce costs, but it also increases dependence on outside partners. This reliance may impact the organization's agility and control over production. Thus, thoroughly evaluating these aspects is essential for making an informed choice that supports the organization's long-term objectives.

Understanding Contracts

When working with external vendors, it's crucial that the agreements are explicitly defined to prevent misunderstandings. These are not just verbal arrangements but are formalized through detailed contracts covering all important aspects of the relationship. The essential question at the heart of any contract is: What are the parties agreeing to, and what exact conditions apply? To ensure clarity and mutual understanding, contracts should clearly define the following elements:

Scope of Work: This section describes the specific services or products the vendor will deliver, including expected outcomes, required specifications for the deliverables, and the partnership's overall goal.

Cost and Payment Terms: This section describes the overall cost of the services, including any applicable fees, taxes, or additional charges. It also explains the payment schedule, indicating whether payments are due upon project completion, at certain milestones, or based on another agreement.

Timeline and Deliverables: A well-structured contract will include a clear project timeline that highlights key milestones and deadlines. This ensures that both parties have a shared understanding of when deliverables are expected, which can help manage performance and expectations.

Responsibilities of Each Party: Contracts should clearly define the roles and responsibilities of both the vendor and the client. This clarity helps each party understand their expectations, promotes accountability, and reduces the risk of misunderstandings.

Creating detailed and transparent contracts builds a strong foundation that reduces misunderstandings. This organized approach enhances accountability and protects the interests of both parties. This results in a more productive and cooperative working relationship.

Common Types of Contracts

In project management, selecting the right contract type is crucial, as it greatly influences project success. Different contracts offer various advantages that improve efficiency and teamwork, as well as certain risks that require careful assessment. Grasping these differences is vital for project managers to manage contractual responsibilities effectively and ensure they support the project's objectives. Below are detailed descriptions of the most common contract types:

Fixed-Price Contracts: This type of contract sets a fixed price for the entire project scope, providing cost certainty since both parties know the total cost upfront. While the buyer gains predictable expenses, the vendor's flexibility to modify the scope or requirements is limited. Fixed-price contracts work best when project requirements are clear and unlikely to change, making them ideal for low-uncertainty projects.

Time and Materials (T&M) Contracts: This contract type specifies that payment depends on the actual hours worked and materials used. T&M contracts offer flexibility, which is useful in situations where project scope may change. However, if not carefully managed, they can result in higher costs due to reduced incentives for efficiency. Precise tracking of time and resources is crucial to avoid exceeding the budget. These contracts are frequently chosen for projects with exploratory work or initially uncertain requirements.

Cost-Reimbursable Contracts: A cost-reimbursable contract means the buyer pays the seller for actual project expenses plus a fee, which can be fixed or a percentage of the total. This approach lowers vendor risk by guaranteeing payment for costs, but raises the buyer's risk due to potential unpredictability and cost overruns. These contracts are well-suited for projects with uncertain or changing scopes, as they permit adjustments when new information emerges.

Selecting the appropriate contract type is vital for a project's success. It requires evaluating the project's uncertainty, specific requirements, scope, risk appetite, and financial factors. Conducting a detailed assessment will support making the most informed choice.

Risks in Procurement

Procurement involves multiple risks due to its dependence on external partners and suppliers. If not properly managed, these risks can significantly affect project schedules, costs, and quality. Typical risks related to procurement include:

Vendor Delays: External vendors may encounter unforeseen circumstances that cause delivery delays. These delays can disrupt project schedules and create bottlenecks in the workflow.

Quality Issues: The procured products or services may not meet the required standards or specifications. Subpar quality could result in additional rework or replacement costs and may also harm the company's reputation.

Miscommunication of Requirements: Unclear or incomplete communication about project requirements can cause vendors to deliver incorrect products or services. This misalignment may result in project delays and lead to additional negotiations or adjustments.

Cost Overruns: Procurement costs sometimes exceed initial budget estimates because of various factors. Market fluctuations can cause sudden price hikes for materials or services. Unexpected expenses might also arise from scope changes or emergency requirements, leading to costs not foreseen during the initial planning stage.

Dependency on Third Parties: Relying on third-party vendors may introduce risks, particularly if they encounter operational issues or financial problems. Such dependence can jeopardize the project's stability and continuity.

To reduce procurement risks, thorough planning and effective communication are essential. Developing strong relationships with suppliers and creating clear contracts can significantly reduce the risk of disruptions. Moreover, establishing contingency plans helps ensure that projects proceed smoothly, even when unforeseen challenges occur.

Managing Vendor Relationships

Procurement involves more than just signing contracts; it also focuses on relationship management. Vendor management primarily addresses the essential question of how to ensure that external partners deliver their services or products efficiently and in line with our objectives. This process requires building strong relationships with vendors, which can be achieved through several key practices:

Clear Communication: Establishing open and transparent communication channels is crucial. This means not just sharing information but also actively discussing challenges, updates, and feedback. Regular meetings and updates help ensure everyone stays aligned.

Defined Expectations: Establish clear and measurable expectations from the beginning, covering project timelines, deliverables, quality standards, and regulatory or compliance needs. Ensuring both parties share an understanding of goals and responsibilities helps to minimize misunderstandings and disputes.

Regular Performance Monitoring: Continuous assessment of vendor performance is essential. This includes establishing key performance indicators (KPIs), performing regular reviews, and using performance scorecards. Monitoring vendor compliance with set standards allows organizations to spot improvement opportunities and resolve issues quickly.

Collaboration and Trust: Building a relationship based on trust fosters a partnership approach rather than a transactional one. Involving vendors in problem-solving conversations and acknowledging their input can result in innovative solutions and improved performance.

Treating vendors as partners fosters a more productive and harmonious working relationship. This collaborative approach improves outcomes and reduces the likelihood of conflicts. Ultimately, such partnerships benefit both parties over time.

Common Procurement Mistakes

When procurement processes are poorly managed, projects frequently encounter significant problems that can impede their progress and success. These issues may include delays in obtaining required resources, budget overruns due to mismanagement, and challenges coordinating with vendors, all of which can threaten the project's timeline and quality of delivery. Several common pitfalls can arise during this phase and may jeopardize the success of the project:

Choosing Vendors Based Solely on Cost: While budget constraints are important, choosing vendors solely on the lowest bid can compromise quality and service. A more comprehensive evaluation that includes reputation, reliability, and past performance is vital to ensure the best overall value.

Failing to Clearly Define Contract Terms: Vague or incomplete contract terms can cause misunderstandings and disputes down the line. It is crucial to clearly specify deliverables, timelines, payment schedules, and penalties for non-compliance to prevent legal problems and ensure both parties have aligned expectations.

Not Monitoring Vendor Performance: After selecting a vendor, it's essential to define key performance indicators (KPIs) and consistently monitor their performance. Regular evaluations enable early detection of problems, facilitating timely corrections and helping to keep the project on track.

Poor Communication with External Partners: Effective communication forms the foundation of successful partnerships. Keeping open communication with vendors helps prevent misunderstandings and promotes collaboration. Regular check-ins and updates foster trust and keep everyone informed and aligned throughout the project.

Over-Reliance on a Single Vendor: Relying on a single vendor for essential components can introduce supply chain risks. Diversifying your vendor base helps mitigate this risk by providing alternative options in the event of delays or quality issues.

To avoid common mistakes, thorough planning is essential for any organization. Implementing diligent oversight and cultivating strong relationship management practices are also key factors. By building collaborative partnerships and adopting a proactive approach, organizations can significantly enhance their procurement processes and increase project success.

Real-World Example: Building a House and Working with Vendors

Imagine you are managing the construction of a house and have already defined the scope, schedule, budget, resources, and risks. At this stage, you realize that not all work can be completed by your internal team.

You may need to hire specialized contractors, such as electricians, plumbers, or roofing experts. You may also need to purchase materials, including lumber, fixtures, and appliances, from external suppliers. Each of these decisions involves procurement.

For instance, you need to choose between hiring a contractor for electrical work or handling it in-house. Hiring a professional guarantees quality and regulatory compliance, though it comes at a cost. Managing the work internally might save money, but could pose risks if the required expertise isn't present.

Once you select a vendor, you must establish clear terms. This includes defining the scope of work, timeline, and payment conditions. If expectations are not clearly communicated, the contractor may deliver work that fails to meet requirements, resulting in delays and additional costs.

Procurement also introduces dependencies. If a supplier fails to deliver materials on time, it can delay multiple tasks in the schedule. Similarly, if a contractor's work does not meet quality standards, it may require rework, which can affect both cost and timeline.

As the project manager, your responsibilities include carefully selecting vendors, establishing clear agreements, and maintaining effective communication throughout the project. By managing procurement effectively, you can ensure that external resources support the project's success rather than introduce risks.

Connecting to Your Project (Project 1)

In this stage of your Project Management Plan, it is essential to specify the particular goods and services needed for the project's success. Additionally, it is important to specify any specialized external expertise required to ensure all aspects are addressed. This clarity facilitates the acquisition process and ensures external resources are aligned with project goals. It involves several essential steps:

Begin with a detailed overview of the specific items, services, or skills required to effectively meet your project's objectives. This could include key software tools for management and communication, high-grade materials for construction or production, expert consulting services providing specialized insights, and skilled labor essential for carrying out various tasks. Clearly specify each requirement to ensure a thorough understanding of what is needed to complete the project successfully.

Assess whether to produce goods or services internally or to outsource them. It's important to consider costs and the time needed for production. Also, review the quality of the final product and the availability of internal resources, as these can greatly impact the decision. A comprehensive evaluation of all these factors will guide you toward the most advantageous choice for the organization.

Determine the most suitable contract type for your vendors, such as fixed-price, time-and-materials, or cost-reimbursable agreements, considering the procurement's nature and associated risks. Develop a framework to monitor and evaluate vendor performance. You achieve this by defining specific performance metrics, conducting regular reviews, and creating feedback systems to ensure the goods or services align with your project's standards.

To enhance the success of your project, it's essential to strategically organize and efficiently manage all external dependencies. By addressing these crucial aspects, you increase the likelihood of achieving your project goals. This proactive approach can lead to significant improvements in overall project performance.

Reflection Questions

Think about a time when you relied on someone outside your team to complete a task. Were the expectations clearly defined? Did they deliver on time and as expected? What would you do differently to improve that experience?

Closing Thought

No project exists in total isolation. Every project, at some stage, relies on external resources, expertise, or materials. Managing these relationships well can be the key to success or failure. As you progress, keep in mind that procurement isn't merely about obtaining resources; it's about forming dependable partnerships that help achieve your project's objectives.

Full Steam Ahead - Process Port

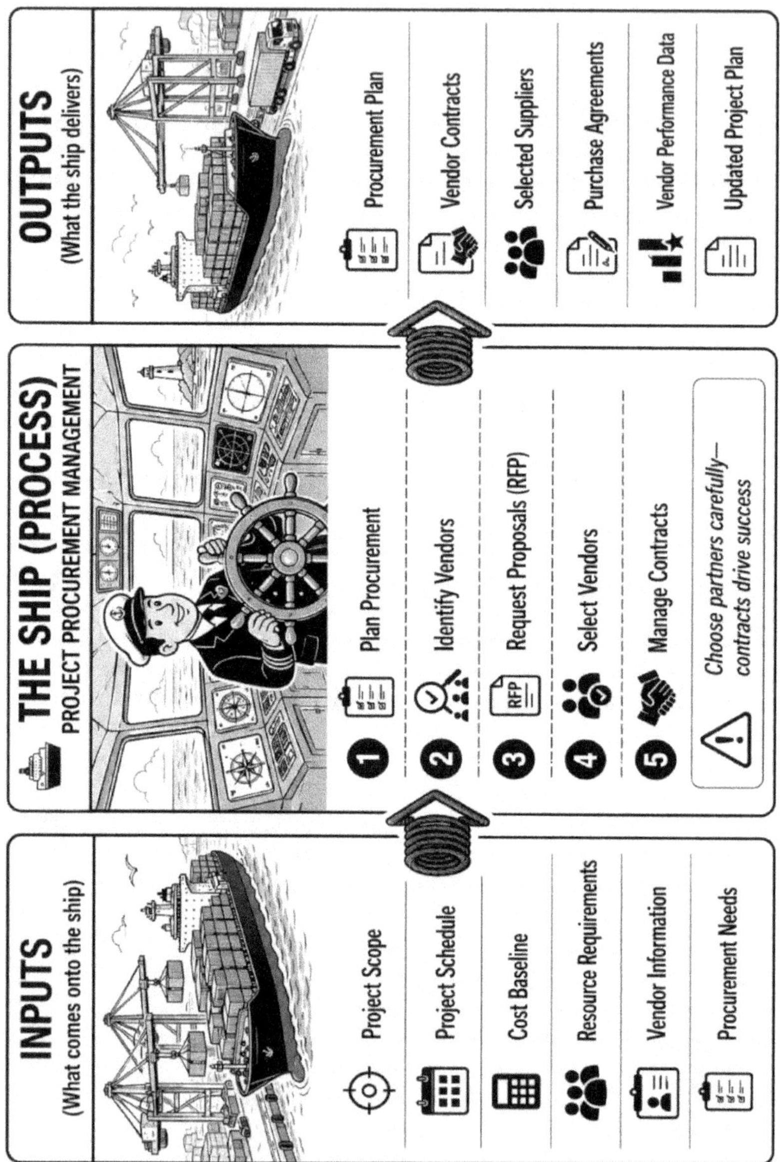

⚓ *Key Takeaways*

✓ Procurement involves acquiring goods and services from external sources

✓ Vendors are used when expertise, capacity, or resources are not available internally

✓ A structured procurement process ensures fairness, clarity, and accountability

✓ Contracts define expectations, responsibilities, and terms of engagement

✓ Strong vendor management helps ensure quality, cost control, and timely delivery

End-of-Chapter Questions

1. What is procurement in project management?
2. Why might a project require external vendors or suppliers?
3. What are the key steps in the procurement process?
4. What is the purpose of a request for proposal (RFP)?
5. What are common types of contracts used in projects?
6. What is the difference between fixed-price and time-and-materials contracts?
7. Why are contracts important in procurement?
8. What risks are associated with working with external vendors?

9. How can a project manager effectively manage vendor relationships?

10. How does procurement impact overall project success?

📖 *Captain's Log: Discussion Board*

Recall a moment when you depended on an external provider, vendor, or service to finish a task or project. What issues did you face regarding communication, expectations, or delivery? Consider how establishing clearer agreements, setting defined expectations, or improving vendor management might have led to a better result.

Chapter 8 - Planning Peninsula

(Project Management Plan)

⌖ Learning Objectives

By the end of this chapter, you should be able to:

- ✓ Understand the purpose of a comprehensive project management plan

- ✓ Identify the key components that make up a project plan

- ✓ Explain how scope, schedule, cost, resources, risk, and procurement integrate into one plan

- ✓ Recognize the importance of aligning all planning elements before execution

- ✓ Understand how a well-developed plan supports successful project delivery

Planning Peninsula

⚓ *Reaching Planning Peninsula*

As the Deliverables continues its journey, the river opens into a wide expanse ahead, a peninsula extending into the water. The currents slow, and the environment grows calm, almost reflective.

Captain Brian signals the crew to pause. "We've reached Planning Peninsula," he says. The crew looks around, noticing that the journey has changed. The urgency of navigating obstacles has given way to a moment of clarity. "What happens here?" one crew member asks.

The captain steps forward. "This is where everything we've prepared comes together." He gestures back toward the river. "We've defined where we're going. We've mapped the path, planned our time, calculated our costs, built our team, prepared for risks, and secured what we need."

The crew nods. "So… we're ready?" another asks.

The captain smiles. "We're close. But before we move forward, we must make sure everything fits together." He pauses. "A plan isn't just a collection of parts, it's a system. And if one part is off, the whole journey can suffer."

What Is a Project Management Plan?

At its core, a Project Management Plan answers a key question: How can we guarantee the project's successful completion from start to finish? It's more than a set of separate documents; it's an integrated framework that encompasses all aspects of project planning. This document serves as a detailed roadmap, guiding the project team through each phase of the project lifecycle, from initiation and planning through execution, monitoring, and closure.

Achieving the project's objectives necessitates a comprehensive approach that considers scope, schedule, cost, quality, resources, risk, and procurement as interconnected elements. The Project Management Plan is crucial for this integration, providing a structured framework. This guarantees that every component works together towards a shared goal and supports each other during the project.

When creating the Project Management Plan, project managers specify clear objectives, precisely define the project scope, develop a detailed schedule to monitor progress, and assign resources efficiently. They incorporate risk management strategies to foresee and address potential issues and set quality standards to ensure deliverables meet or surpass expectations. Furthermore, the plan includes procurement strategies outlining how external resources and services will be sourced and managed.

The Project Management Plan is a living document that adapts as the project progresses. It serves as an essential reference for all stakeholders, informing decision-making. Effective communication within the team ensures everyone stays aligned and focused on achieving the project's specific objectives.

Integrating the Plan Components

Up to this point, each chapter has focused on a specific aspect of planning. Now, those elements must be connected.

A strong Project Management Plan integrates:

- **Scope:** What will be done

- **Schedule:** When it will be done

- **Cost:** How much it will cost

- **Quality:** How well it must be done

- **Resources:** Who and what is needed

- **Risk:** What uncertainties may arise

- **Procurement:** What must be obtained externally

Each component influences the others. A change in scope may affect the schedule and cost. A risk may affect resources or procurement. These relationships must be understood and managed.

Alignment and Consistency

A successful plan depends significantly on how well its parts work together. Central to this idea is the principle of alignment, which can be summarized with one key question: Are all elements working together to support the overall goal? Achieving this alignment is essential to ensure that every component contributes effectively, resulting in a unified strategy that promotes success.

For example, if the schedule is aggressive, are sufficient resources allocated? If the budget is limited, is the scope realistic? If the risks are high, are contingency plans in place? Misalignment can create gaps that lead to delays, increased costs, and quality issues.

Identifying Gaps in the Plan

Before advancing to the next stages of the project, the project manager must meticulously review the entire project plan. This thorough review should focus on identifying any inconsistencies, ambiguities, or missing components that could hinder progress or lead to complications down the line. Common gaps include:

- Tasks in the schedule that are not defined in scope

- Costs that are not tied to specific activities

- Risks that have no response strategy

- Resources assigned without clear roles

- Procurement needs that are not planned

Recognizing and resolving shortcomings early is crucial for avoiding bigger problems during implementation. By proactively addressing these gaps, we can streamline the process. In the end, this strategy results in better long-term outcomes.

The Role of Integration

Integration is an essential aspect of project management that guarantees all project components work together smoothly and efficiently as a single system. Essentially, it answers the key question: How do these individual parts collaborate to fulfill the project's goals?

To achieve successful integration, project managers need to facilitate ongoing coordination among team members, stakeholders, and various project elements. This involves not only aligning tasks and resources but also maintaining open communication and collaboration throughout each phase. Effective integration requires a flexible and adaptable approach, allowing the project to evolve while maintaining overall cohesion.

As the project develops, changes are unavoidable, and the project manager is key in evaluating their impacts. Every adjustment can affect the entire project, requiring a reassessment of the overall plan to preserve its integrity. This involves a proactive strategy, with the project manager regularly reviewing how all components fit together to ensure they stay aligned with common goals despite shifts in scope, schedule, or resources.

For example, a delay in procurement can significantly impact the entire project schedule, shifting timelines and possibly postponing deliverables. Likewise, a change in the budget can greatly affect the project's scope, potentially reducing the quality or amount of outputs. Additionally, an unexpected risk event may require reassigning resources, disrupting initial planning and execution. Proper management of integration across all project components is essential to keep the project balanced, coherent, and aligned with its original goals and objectives.

Common Planning Mistakes

Even projects with good initial intentions may fail if the planning stage lacks careful thought and thoroughness. Proper planning is essential; without it, even the most promising ideas can stumble and fall. Common mistakes include:

- Treating planning components as separate rather than integrated

- Failing to review the full plan before execution

- Ignoring inconsistencies between scope, schedule, and cost

- Overlooking risks or procurement dependencies

- Rushing into execution without validating the plan

Avoiding these mistakes requires discipline and attention to detail.

Connecting to Your Project (Project 1)

At this stage, you are finalizing your Project Management Plan. You should now have:

- A clearly defined scope

- A structured schedule

- A cost estimate and budget

- Defined quality expectations

- Identified resources and roles

- A risk management plan

- A procurement strategy (if applicable)

Your goal is to review your entire plan and ensure that all components are aligned and complete.

Reflection Questions

Reflect on a time when you carefully planned something, yet problems still emerged during execution. Was your plan fully aligned? Did you overlook any crucial elements? What changes would you make to ensure everything integrates smoothly?

Closing Thought

A solid plan doesn't ensure success, but a weak one almost certainly leads to failure. Investing time to integrate and align all aspects of your Project Management Plan builds a strong foundation for execution. Once you leave Planning Peninsula, you're no longer preparing; you're ready to start the journey.

Full Steam Ahead - Process Port

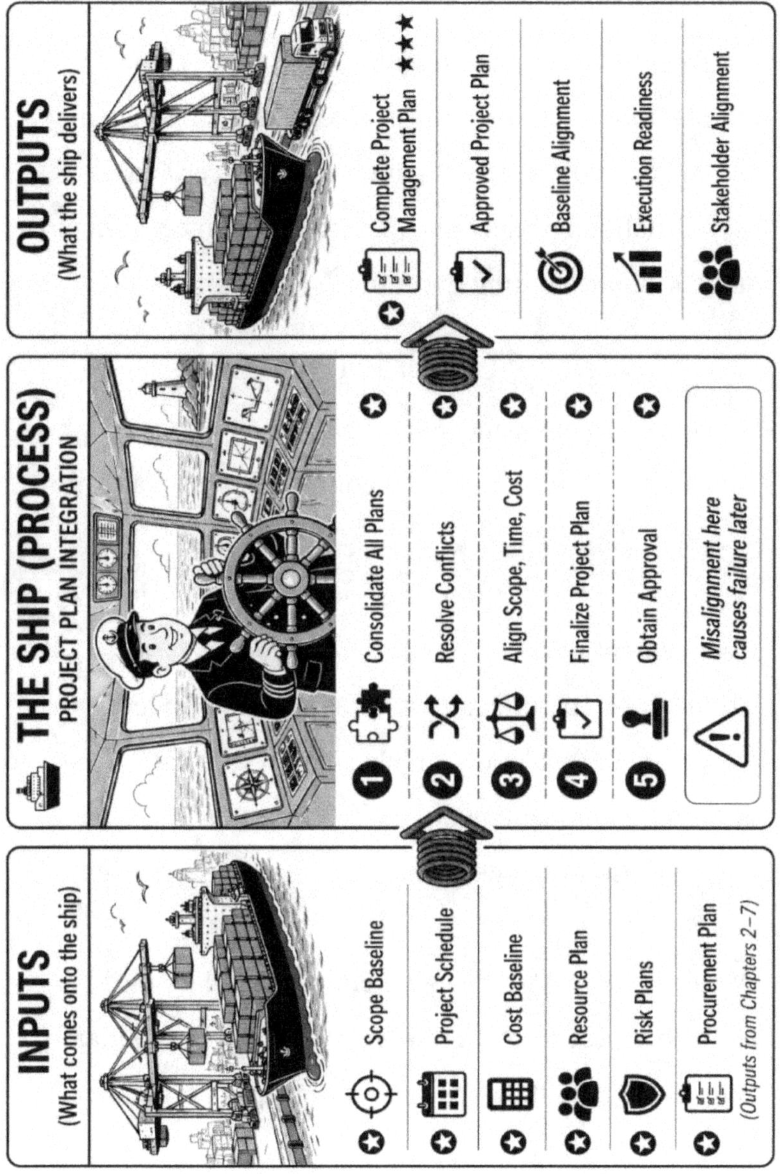

⚓ *Key Takeaways*

✓ The project management plan serves as the main document guiding the execution.

✓ All planning sections must be integrated and aligned

✓ Having a detailed project plan reduces uncertainty

✓ A well-defined project plan provides guidance, structure, and confidence during execution.

End-of-Chapter Questions

1. What is a project management plan?

2. Why is it important to have a comprehensive plan before execution begins?

3. What are the key components included in a project management plan?

4. How does scope integrate into the overall project plan?

5. How does the project schedule support the plan?

6. Why is cost management crucial in the planning phase?

7. How do resources and communication fit into the project plan?

8. What role does risk management play in planning?

9. How does procurement integrate into the overall plan?

10. Why is alignment across all planning areas critical before execution begins?

▱ *Captain's Log: Discussion Board*

Recall a moment when you began a task or project without thorough planning. What obstacles did you encounter while executing it? Consider how a comprehensive and well-coordinated plan might have enhanced teamwork, minimized confusion, and led to a more successful outcome.

Congratulations! You've completed the first half of the book and finished Project 1: The Project Management Plan.

FULL STEAM AHEAD:
→ PROJECT MAP (2nd HALF) ←
N
W E
S
CHAPTER 16:
FINISH LINE
CHAPTER 15:
CLOSING DOCK
CHAPTER 14:
ACCOUNTABILITY
ANCHORAGE
CHAPTER 13:
AGILE
ARCHIPELAGO
CHAPTER 12:
LEADERSHIP
LOOKOUT
CHAPTER 11:
CONTROL
TOWER WATERS
CHAPTER 10:
EXECUTION
BAY
DELIVERABLES
WELCOME BACK
CHAPTER 9:
PMI ISLAND

Welcome Back

You've come a long way.

In the first half of this journey, you didn't just learn about project management; you built something real. Gradually, you crafted a comprehensive Project Management Plan, which gave you a solid grasp of how projects are organized, scheduled, and set up for success. You linked the elements, understood how decisions influence results, and laid a foundational groundwork that most don't often bother to establish.

Now, we shift course.

The next phase moves from planning to execution and leadership. You will explore how projects are carried out through Project Execution, how progress is tracked and adjusted via Monitoring and Controlling, and how projects are finalized with Project Closing. Additionally, you'll learn about Agile methodologies and leadership principles, gaining skills to guide teams, adapt to change, and deliver results in real-world scenarios.

At the same time, this section introduces a second, equally important focus on your own experience.

As you progress through the upcoming chapters, you'll start converting your real-world tasks into project management terminology. You'll reflect on your actions, identify the specific tasks you've completed, and align them with the relevant project management process groups. This process will help you communicate your experiences more clearly and professionally, transforming routine work into a well-structured and recognized project experience.

This dual focus is intentional.

You are not only learning how to execute and lead projects, but also how to show that you've already been part of that process. Many professionals have the experience necessary for career growth but find it hard to articulate it. They know they've contributed, solved issues, and achieved results, but lack the framework to present that experience confidently. This next phase aims to change that.

By the end of this journey, you'll gain more than just knowledge. You'll possess a documented record of your experience, a better understanding of how projects function in real-world settings, and the ability to link your work to established project management practices. Whether you aim for certification, career growth, or to become more effective in your role, this section prepares you to proceed with clarity and confidence.

You already possess more experience than you realize, and you're not starting from scratch. This next stage focuses on clarifying that experience, organizing it into a clear structure, and learning to communicate it intentionally. At the same time, you'll keep developing as someone who can execute, lead, and deliver effectively.

Your efforts have led you to this point. The plan is in place, and now it's time to execute it.

Project 2 – Project Experience

While the first half of this journey focused on planning the voyage, the second half emphasizes something just as important: understanding and documenting your experience as a project manager.

Many people complete projects but struggle to describe their experience in a way that meets professional standards. This is especially important when pursuing certifications such as the Project Management Professional (PMP), which require documenting project experience.

This project is designed to help you bridge that gap.

Purpose of This Project

Throughout Chapters 9 through 16, you will start creating your Project Experience Log, a structured method for documenting your work using the five Project Management Process Groups.

- Initiating

- Planning

- Executing

- Monitoring and Controlling

- Closing

As you move through each chapter, you'll think about real projects from school, work, or personal life, and start converting those experiences into professional project management terminology.

Why This Matters

Many people already have project experience; they just haven't realized it yet.

You may have:

- Led a team project

- Coordinated an event

- Managed a deadline-driven task

- Worked in a role with responsibilities tied to outcomes

The challenge is not gaining experience; it is learning how to articulate it.

This project will help you:

- Recognize your existing experience

- Organize your work into structured categories

- Align your experience with PMP requirements

- Prepare for future certification applications

Seeing Your Work Differently

One common misconception about project management experience is that only official "project manager" roles count. That isn't correct. Projects happen all around you every day in many different jobs. A project is simply a temporary effort to create a unique result. From this point of view, many kinds of work can be considered project experience.

Projects Exist in Every Profession

No matter what your background is, you have likely already contributed to projects. Examples include:

Retail & Sales

- Seasonal sales campaigns

- Store layout redesigns

- Monthly or quarterly sales targets

Janitorial & Operations

- Facility deep cleaning initiatives

- Scheduled maintenance cycles

- Compliance or inspection preparation

Technology & Software Development

- Feature releases

- System upgrades

- Bug fix cycles and sprint work

Education & Teaching

- Semester-based course delivery

- Curriculum development

- Student performance initiatives

Business & Administration

- Quarterly reporting cycles

- Process improvements

- Internal initiatives or rollouts

Each of these examples has:

- A beginning and an end

- A defined objective

- Measurable outcomes

That makes them projects.

Shift: From "Job Tasks" to "Project Experience"

Most people describe their work as, "I helped customers, completed daily tasks, and followed procedures." But in project management language, that same experience becomes, "Participated in seasonal sales initiative, supported execution of promotional strategy, and contributed to achieving quarterly revenue targets."

The work did not change. ***The way it is described did.***

Understanding Time, the PMI Way

Another key concept is how "experience" is measured. Organizations like PMI assess project experience based on time spent working on projects, usually measured in months, which is then converted into project hours.

This means:

- Work done repeatedly (daily/weekly) can be grouped into a single project

- Ongoing responsibilities can be organized into time-bound initiatives

- Experience is calculated based on how long you were involved

For example:

- A retail employee working during the holiday seasons each year

- A teacher delivering courses each semester

- A developer contributing to quarterly releases

Each of these can be translated into project experience measured over time.

Your Role in This Process

Your goal in this project is to:

✓ Identify work you have already done

✓ Group that work into meaningful "projects."

✓ Define the timeframe of each project

✓ Describe your role using project management language

✓ Map your experience to the five process groups

It's important to accurately recognize the impact of your previous work. This involves communicating the value you bring without exaggeration. This helps you clearly showcase your true contributions and achievements.

Your Objective

By the end of Chapter 16, you will have created a personal Project Experience Log that includes:

- A summary of one or more real projects

- Your role in each project

- Tasks mapped to the five process groups

- Clear, professional descriptions of your duties

How This Project Works

Each chapter in the second half of this book will guide you through one part of documenting your experience.

You will:

1. Reflect on real work you have completed

2. Identify tasks you performed

3. Map those tasks to a process group

4. Write clear, professional descriptions

By the end, you will have a document that can act as a basis for: PMP application, resume enhancements, and interview preparation

⌓ *Captain's Reminder*

You're not starting from zero; you already possess more experience than you think. This project focuses on helping you recognize and express that experience. You're developing the ability to translate your existing work experience into project experience that is understood worldwide.

Scan to Download your
Experience Project Template:

Project 2 – Experience Log Checklist

Initiating Experience

- ☐ Identify tasks related to starting the project
- ☐ Describe how the project began
- ☐ Document your involvement in defining goals or scope

Planning Experience

- ☐ Identify planning-related tasks you performed
- ☐ Describe scheduling or organizing activities
- ☐ Document tools or methods used

Executing Experience

- ☐ Identify tasks where work was carried out
- ☐ Describe coordination or task execution
- ☐ Document team involvement

Monitoring & Controlling Experience

- ☐ Identify how progress was tracked
- ☐ Describe issue resolution or adjustments made
- ☐ Document how performance was measured

Closing Experience

- ☐ Identify how the project or work concluded
- ☐ Describe deliverables or outcomes

Final Deliverable

- ☐ Compile experience into a structured format
- ☐ Review for clarity and professionalism
- ☐ Save for future certification use

Chapter 9 – PMI Island

(Exploring the PMI Framework)

Learning Objectives

By the end of this chapter, you should be able to:

- ✓ Understand the role of the Project Management Institute (PMI)
- ✓ Explain the purpose of project management standards and frameworks
- ✓ Identify the key components of the PMBOK® Guide at a high level
- ✓ Recognize the value of professional certifications such as the PMP®
- ✓ Understand how PMI supports the growth and development of project managers

CHAPTER 9

PMI Island

⚓ *Arriving at PMI Island*

As the Deliverables continues its journey, the river opens into a vast shoreline unlike anything the crew has seen before. Palm trees line the coast, and large structures rise in the distance, organized, orderly, and well-established.

Captain Brian brings the vessel to a slow stop. "We've arrived at PMI Island," he announces.

The crew looks around, noticing that everything here seems… standardized. "What is this place?" one crew member asks.

The captain steps forward. "This is where project management is studied, defined, and refined. Everything we've been doing, including scope, schedule, cost, and resources, connects back to the principles developed here."

Another crew member looks puzzled. "So… have we been doing it right?"

The captain smiles. "You've been doing it right. Now you're going to understand *why*."

He gestures toward the island. "This is where experience meets structure."

What Is PMI?

At its core, the Project Management Institute (PMI) addresses a fundamental question: How can we define, standardize, and enhance project management practices across industries? As a leading global organization, PMI plays a pivotal role in shaping the future of project management by developing comprehensive standards, certifications, and best practices tailored to project management professionals at all levels.

PMI aims to offer a unified language and framework that helps project managers in various industries communicate and collaborate effectively. This shared framework aligns all stakeholders, making discussions and decision-making smoother. Using consistent practices allows project managers to standardize their methods, greatly increasing the chances of project success.

The organization draws on extensive research and practical experience to provide guidance that helps professionals manage project complexities without repeatedly reinventing their approach. By emphasizing established best practices, it supports project managers in achieving successful results and enhances overall efficiency, risk management, and stakeholder engagement.

PMI's contributions are essential for individuals and organizations aiming to improve their project management skills. By offering a wealth of resources, training, and best practices, PMI empowers project managers to navigate complex challenges and lead their teams to success. This increase in capabilities not only deepens understanding of project complexities but also supports the successful delivery of projects aligned with their organizations' strategic aims. In the end, PMI's initiatives and backing facilitate more effective project results, promoting organizational growth and innovation.

Understanding the PMBOK® Guide

One of the Project Management Institute (PMI)'s most significant contributions to the field of project management is the development of the **PMBOK® Guide**, the Project Management Body of Knowledge. This guide is an essential resource for project managers across industries. By providing standardized practices and processes, it helps ensure successful project execution.

The PMBOK® Guide fundamentally answers a key question for many professionals: What are the most effective project management practices? It leverages extensive industry knowledge and research to compile proven strategies and techniques to ensure successful project completion.

The PMBOK® Guide isn't meant to be a rigid, step-by-step manual enforcing a single project management approach. Instead, it offers a flexible framework of principles, processes, and guidelines, enabling project managers to tailor their methods and workflows to meet each project's specific needs.

By offering a structured approach, the PMBOK® guide provides clarity and direction while enabling adaptability. This flexibility is crucial because projects often have varying scopes, objectives, and challenges. Consequently, project managers can use the PMBOK® Guide to craft a customized project management strategy that aligns with the specific requirements and context of their initiatives. Ultimately, the PMBOK® Guide enhances the effectiveness and efficiency of project management practices worldwide.

Process Groups: The Project Lifecycle

The Project Management Institute (PMI) has defined a systematic approach to project work by categorizing it into five distinct process groups. These groups collectively represent the full lifecycle of a project, guiding managers through key phases from start to finish. Each process group is vital to ensuring projects are carried out efficiently and successfully, helping teams handle the complexities of project management. Each group plays a distinct role and is essential to achieving successful project results.

Initiating: This process focuses on outlining the project at a high level, assessing its feasibility, and setting its scope. It involves obtaining stakeholder approvals, defining key objectives, and identifying initial resource needs. The purpose of initiation is to ensure a clear understanding of the project's scope and to gain the commitment necessary to proceed.

Planning: This process involves creating a comprehensive project execution plan. It includes defining the project scope, developing a timeline, allocating resources, and setting budgets. Risks are identified, mitigation strategies are planned, and progress-tracking methods are implemented. Overall, planning carefully considers and organizes every aspect of the project to ensure successful delivery.

Executing: This process is where the project's core work occurs. It includes coordinating personnel and resources, managing stakeholder expectations, and ensuring deliverables align with the project plan. Effective communication is crucial at this stage. Ongoing collaboration and troubleshooting are essential for keeping the project on track.

Monitoring and Controlling: This process runs in parallel with execution and monitors the project's progress against the plan. It involves assessing performance, identifying variances, and making adjustments to keep the project on track toward its objectives. This process helps address potential problems quickly, preserving stakeholder confidence and maintaining the project's integrity.

Closing: The final process of the project lifecycle involves wrapping up all activities to formally close the project. This includes securing stakeholder approval of deliverables, releasing project resources, performing a post-project review, and recording lessons learned. The closing phase ensures a proper conclusion and provides useful insights for future projects.

These process groups in the PMBOK® closely mirror the journey you've been following in this book, highlighting the essential stages and tasks that guide a project from its initial conception to final completion. Each process is designed to ensure careful management and execution of every aspect of the project. This framework promotes achieving successful and efficient results, guiding the project to completion.

Knowledge Areas: The Areas of Focus

The Project Management Institute (PMI) provides a detailed framework with multiple process groups and knowledge areas essential to successful project management. These areas include core components that help project managers and teams navigate complex challenges across every project phase. By understanding and applying these knowledge areas, teams can improve their planning, execution, and goal achievement, ensuring all key aspects are properly addressed and managed. They include:

Scope Management: This knowledge area focuses on clearly defining and controlling the project's boundaries, specifying what is within and outside its scope. It involves detailed planning, with each deliverable clearly described to ensure all stakeholders share a shared understanding of the project's goals and objectives. This common understanding helps the team coordinate their efforts more effectively and increases the likelihood of success.

Schedule Management: This knowledge area focuses on creating and managing a detailed project timeline that serves as a guide throughout the project. It involves identifying specific tasks, organizing them logically to facilitate an efficient workflow, and estimating how long each will take. Regular tracking of progress against this timeline is essential to ensure the project stays on schedule and finishes on time. By closely monitoring these elements, the project manager can proactively address potential delays and steer the project toward successful completion.

Cost Management: This knowledge area focuses on estimating costs, developing budgets, and tracking expenses to ensure the project stays within its financial limits. It involves carefully reviewing all project-related costs and making detailed forecasts to predict future financial requirements. By carefully analyzing these financial aspects, project managers can effectively allocate resources, control expenses, and make informed decisions to improve the project's success while maintaining financial discipline.

Quality Management: This knowledge area focuses on a comprehensive approach to guarantee that the project consistently adheres to quality standards throughout its lifecycle. It includes detailed planning of quality assurance methods to prevent defects and align with project objectives. Additionally, it encompasses implementing quality control measures, such as systematic reviews and inspections at various stages, to identify and resolve issues early. Continuous monitoring is essential, involving regular evaluation of performance metrics and stakeholder feedback to ensure expectations are met, ultimately fostering high stakeholder satisfaction.

Resource Management: This knowledge area focuses on the systematic identification, acquisition, and management of both human and physical resources essential for successfully executing the project. It encompasses various aspects such as fostering team development, strategically allocating resources, and implementing effective performance management practices. The ultimate goal is to optimize overall efficiency and ensure each resource is used to its fullest potential, thereby facilitating smooth project execution and enhancing team productivity.

Communications Management: This knowledge area focuses on a comprehensive approach to planning, implementing, and overseeing communication strategies. It is designed to ensure that all stakeholders, including team members, clients, and other interested parties, are well-informed and actively engaged throughout the project. By establishing clear channels and methods for information exchange, this process facilitates the smooth flow of relevant updates, feedback, and important announcements, ensuring seamless communication throughout the project's lifecycle.

Risk Management: This knowledge area focuses on thoroughly identifying potential risks that could threaten the project's success. This involves not only identifying these risks but also conducting a thorough analysis to assess their potential impact and likelihood of occurrence. After the risk assessment, developing effective mitigation strategies is crucial. Proactively managing risks helps reduce disruptions and challenges, increasing the likelihood of meeting project goals. This approach not only protects the project from unexpected problems but also promotes a more stable and successful outcome.

Procurement Management: This knowledge area focuses on the strategic acquisition of goods and services from external providers to meet specific needs. It encompasses a comprehensive process that includes meticulous planning of purchases, executing procurement activities, and fostering strong vendor relationships. These steps are essential to ensuring that the resources acquired effectively support the successful delivery of project objectives.

Stakeholder Management: This knowledge area focuses on the importance of actively engaging with and managing the expectations of all stakeholders involved in or affected by the project. It includes a comprehensive process of identifying stakeholders such as team members, clients, suppliers, and community members. By understanding their specific needs, concerns, and goals, the project team can customize its approach to effectively address these interests. The approach also emphasizes maintaining transparent and open communication, fostering collaboration, and keeping all parties informed and involved throughout the project. Ultimately, this builds trust and alignment, contributing to a successful project outcome.

Integration Management: This knowledge area focuses on coordinating a project's components to ensure smooth integration and operation. It involves developing the project charter, which specifies the project's vision and scope, along with a detailed project management plan that guides execution. Moreover, it highlights the importance of ongoing monitoring and adjustments throughout the project lifecycle to keep performance aligned with set goals. By encouraging collaboration and communication among team members and stakeholders, this approach aims to boost project success and deliver results.

Each knowledge area focuses on a particular aspect of project management, and effective integration and collaboration among them are essential for achieving project success. A project manager needs to understand the details of each knowledge area and how they connect and support one another. This comprehensive approach helps manage the complexities of project delivery and ensures all parts work together smoothly to achieve project objectives. Mastering and integrating these areas is essential for any project manager aiming for successful and meaningful results.

How Process Groups and Knowledge Areas Work Together

The core of project management centers around a key question: how do we successfully utilize different knowledge areas at each phase of the project lifecycle? This relationship is key to ensuring smooth and successful project execution.

In project management, process groups and knowledge areas serve distinct yet interrelated purposes. Process groups define the sequence and timing of activities, ensuring that each phase of a project flows smoothly and effectively from one stage to the next. Knowledge areas, in turn, provide a structured framework that identifies and organizes the aspects that need to be overseen throughout the project, such as scope, cost, and quality management. Together, these elements create a comprehensive approach that enhances project planning and execution, helping teams achieve their objectives efficiently.

For example, in the Planning phase of a project, the scope is carefully defined. This step is important because it creates a detailed framework that helps all stakeholders fully understand the project's goals and deliverables. Clearly defining what needs to be achieved helps set expectations, clarify roles, and ensure all team members are aligned, paving the way for successful project execution.

Similarly, risk management is an ongoing, active process that plays a vital role during the Monitoring and Controlling phase of a project. This stage involves more than just identifying and assessing potential risks; it also includes proactively developing and implementing strategies to mitigate them as the project progresses. By regularly evaluating threats and vulnerabilities, project managers can adjust their strategies and respond efficiently to new challenges that may emerge throughout the project's lifespan.

During the Execution phase of a project, effective resource management is vital. This complex process requires careful allocation and monitoring of key resources, such as personnel, materials, and finances. Strategic distribution of these resources helps project managers conduct activities efficiently, ensuring the team stays on schedule and within budget. Proper oversight not only boosts productivity but also reduces risks, paving the way for successful project completion.

To successfully manage complex projects, it's crucial to understand how process groups connect with different knowledge areas. This deep understanding helps project managers apply the right tools and techniques precisely when needed. Adopting this strategic approach greatly improves the likelihood of project success. It enables timely adjustments and supports informed decision-making throughout the project lifecycle, leading to more efficient operations and better overall results.

Connecting PMI to Your Project Management Plan

By now, you have developed a complete Project Management Plan through Chapters 1–8. What you may not have realized is that you have been applying PMI principles all along.

Your work has included:

- Defining scope (Scope Management)

- Building a schedule (Schedule Management)

- Estimating costs (Cost Management)

- Managing quality (Quality Management)

- Planning resources and communication (Resource & Communications Management)

- Identifying risks (Risk Management)

- Planning procurement (Procurement Management)

You have effectively created a PMI-aligned plan without memorizing the framework.

Common Misconceptions About PMI

Many people misunderstand PMI, the **PMBOK® Guide,** and their roles in project management.

Common misconceptions include:

PMI is too rigid and not practical

- (false) PMI offers a flexible framework that can be tailored to suit various project requirements, instead of being overly rigid.

The PMBOK® Guide must be followed step-by-step

- (false) The PMBOK® Guide acts as a flexible reference rather than a rigid manual, enabling project managers to adapt their methods according to the specific needs of each project.

PMI only applies to large or complex projects

- (false) PMI methodologies are applicable to projects of all sizes, including small and simple projects, not just large or complex ones.

Real-world projects do not align with PMI

- (false) PMI principles are designed to accommodate real-world project variations, helping teams apply best practices to diverse project environments.

In reality, PMI and the PMBOK® Guide offer a flexible framework. It provides guidance rather than strict rules. Effective project managers adapt these principles to fit their specific situations.

Real-World Example: Aligning a House Project with PMI

Imagine you are in charge of managing the construction of a beautiful new house. You've already crafted a detailed Project Management Plan to guide the process. You now need to ensure that your approach aligns with the standards set by the Project Management Institute (PMI).

To start, you carefully map your existing plan to reflect PMI concepts. Your defined project scope, which outlines the house's specific features and requirements, directly aligns with PMI's Scope Management processes. Similarly, your project timeline, which includes all key milestones and deadlines for each phase of construction, aligns with Schedule Management principles. In terms of finances, you've established a comprehensive budget that tracks expenses and allocations, ensuring it aligns with PMI's Cost Management guidelines.

Your meticulous planning encompasses detailed resource assignments, specifying the personnel, equipment, and materials required for the project. This aligns with Resource Management, ensuring every component has sufficient support. Furthermore, you have developed a comprehensive communication plan that outlines how updates, changes, and critical information will be communicated among team members and stakeholders, which is part of Communications Management.

As the construction advances, you continuously assess risks that could affect the project's success, monitor the overall progress against your schedule, and adjust plans as needed to stay on track. These proactive actions are part of the Monitoring and Controlling processes, demonstrating your dedication to keeping the project under control.

During project closure, holding a lessons learned session is essential. It reviews successes, identifies areas for improvement, and collects stakeholder feedback to refine processes. Documenting these insights preserves valuable knowledge for growth and success. This final stage fits within the Closing process group, ensuring a complete and orderly project closure.

This exercise shows Project Management Institute PMI standards are closely tied to real project management, forming a framework that reflects the proven practices of experienced managers across industries. They embody strategies essential for success, illustrating practical application of theoretical principles.

Connecting to Your Project: Transition to Project 2

With your Project Management Plan complete, you are ready to move into the next phase of your learning journey. In the chapters ahead, you will focus on execution, monitoring, leadership, and real-world application.

You will also start working on Project 2 – The Experience Project, which involves translating real-world tasks into project experience. This chapter acts as a link between planning and execution, guiding you to see how your work aligns with industry standards.

Reflection Questions

Reflect on a process or system you've used in the past. Did it follow a structured approach, even if you didn't realize it? How might applying a standardized framework improve consistency and results? What benefits come from having a shared language across teams and organizations?

Closing Thought

Standards don't limit creativity; they provide a framework for success. PMI offers a structure that connects experience with best practices, helping project managers work confidently. Now that we are leaving PMI Island, you gain knowledge and a better understanding of your role within the broader field.

⚓ *Key Takeaways*

✓ PMI is a leading global organization for project management professionals

✓ Standards like the PMBOK® Guide provide structured guidance and best practices

✓ Project management frameworks help create consistency across industries

✓ Certifications such as the PMP® validate knowledge and experience

End-of-Chapter Questions

1. What is the Project Management Institute (PMI)?
2. What is the purpose of PMI in the project management profession?
3. What is the PMBOK® Guide?
4. Why are project management standards important?
5. What are the knowledge areas in project management?
6. What is the purpose of a project management certification?
7. What is the PMP® certification, and why is it valuable?
8. How does PMI support professional development?
9. Why is it important for project managers to follow established frameworks?
10. How does PMI contribute to consistency and quality in project management practices?

📖 *Captain's Log: Discussion Board*

Consider a profession or field that demands standards, certifications, or best practices. How do these requirements impact performance, credibility, and trust in that area? Reflect on how implementing structured frameworks like those from PMI can enhance consistency and results in project management.

Chapter 10 – Execution Bay
(Project Execution)

🎯 *Learning Objectives*

By the end of this chapter, you should be able to:

- ✓ Understand the purpose of the execution phase in project management
- ✓ Identify key activities involved in executing a project plan
- ✓ Explain the role of leadership during execution
- ✓ Recognize the importance of communication and coordination
- ✓ Understand how deliverables are produced and managed during execution

CHAPTER 10

Execution Bay

⚓ *Entering Execution Bay*

As the *Deliverables* leaves PMI Island, the river opens into a wide, active harbor. Ships move in all directions, crews work together, and the calm reflection of Planning gives way to the constant motion of action.

Captain Brian stands firmly at the helm. "We've entered Execution Bay," he announces.

The crew looks around as activity increases across the ship. "So, this is where we follow the plan?" one crew member asks.

The captain nods, but with a serious expression. "This is where we bring the plan to life."

The crew begins moving into position.

"Planning gave us direction," the captain continues. "Execution gives us results."

He pauses. "But don't expect everything to go exactly as planned."

The crew exchanges glances.

"Because it won't."

What Is Project Execution?

Project execution is a critical phase in the project management process, fundamentally addressing the question: How do we effectively implement our plan to achieve real and measurable results? During this stage, the strategies and objectives outlined in the Project Management Plan are put into action.

In this phase, multiple key activities unfold, including:

Task Execution: Teams fully engage in their assigned tasks, carefully following the timelines and methods developed during planning. Each member contributes their special skills and knowledge, working together to overcome challenges and meet goals. This teamwork improves overall efficiency and creates a space for innovative ideas to develop.

Resource Utilization: To meet the project's goals, resources such as skilled personnel, advanced technology, and financial assets are strategically allocated. Proper management of these resources is essential to ensure they are used effectively and efficiently, minimizing waste and boosting productivity. This careful oversight plays a key role in the overall success of the project.

Constant Communication: Effective interaction in communication channels is essential during project execution. Maintaining a steady schedule of updates, meetings, and detailed reports helps keep all stakeholders informed about progress, potential challenges, and changes to the plan. This ongoing communication fosters collaboration and enables the team to quickly address any issues, facilitating a smoother path to project completion.

Visible Progress: As each task is completed successfully, the project's deliverables become visible evidence of progress and achievement. By carefully monitoring and tracking our progress against set milestones, teams can celebrate successes and identify areas for adjustment or improvement. This continuous review promotes a sense of achievement and helps us stay flexible in responding to any challenges that may emerge.

Ultimately, project execution serves as a bridge between thorough planning and real-world outcomes. It converts well-designed strategies into practical actions, helping to realize the project's goals. This stage not only confirms that the intended objectives are met but also highlights the success of the initial planning, illustrating how ideas can develop into successful implementation.

The Role of the Project Manager During Execution

During the execution phase of a project, the project manager's role shifts from primarily planning to actively leading and coordinating the team's efforts. This transition is crucial because it directly affects the project's success and overall efficiency. This role is centered around a key question: How do we keep all aspects of the project moving forward effectively and in sync?

The project manager has a range of responsibilities that are essential to the project's progress:

Coordinating Team Activities: The project manager is essential for aligning team efforts, ensuring everyone works toward common goals. This includes scheduling regular meetings for open communication, delegating tasks based on individual strengths, and adjusting plans to meet evolving project needs. These actions help sustain progress and promote a collaborative environment that guides the team to success.

Managing Resources: Effective management of resources is crucial for sustaining a project's momentum. The project manager oversees resource allocation, including personnel and materials, ensuring tasks are assigned along with the necessary tools, technology, and support for team members to work efficiently. By promoting collaboration and productivity, the project manager helps individuals realize their full potential, which contributes to the overall success of the project.

Facilitating Communication: Clear and open communication is vital in any project setting, making sure everyone stays aligned and works together toward shared objectives. The project manager acts as the key communicator, enabling effective conversations among team members, stakeholders, and leadership. Regular updates and feedback mechanisms help keep all involved informed, promoting engagement and dedication. This continuous exchange boosts teamwork, builds trust, and encourages responsibility, ultimately guiding the project to success.

Resolving Issues: During any project, various challenges and obstacles are likely to appear, each creating unique hurdles that can affect progress. The project manager's role is to identify these issues promptly, with attention to detail and a sense of urgency. By working closely with the team, the project manager should foster open communication to brainstorm and develop innovative solutions for each problem. This proactive problem-solving approach is essential because it minimizes disruptions and keeps the project moving forward, helping ensure it stays on track and achieves its goals efficiently.

Keeping Work Aligned with the Plan: During a project's execution phase, the project manager is essential in ensuring the team stays aligned with the overall plan and goals. This involves carefully tracking progress against key milestones, which indicate how well the project is advancing. The project manager should monitor these benchmarks closely and be ready to make quick, informed adjustments to keep the project on course for success. By actively collaborating with the team and offering guidance, the project manager helps overcome challenges, keeping the project on track and aligned with its objectives.

As the team diligently works to finish their tasks, the project manager acts as the keystone of the project's progress. With careful attention to detail, they oversee and steer vital functions, making sure each team member stays aligned and motivated. By encouraging collaboration and open communication, the project manager helps overcome challenges and ensures the project moves forward smoothly toward successful completion.

Managing *Work and Deliverables*

Execution is more than just beginning tasks; it requires careful and efficient completion aligned with specific objectives. For a task to be considered successful, it must fulfill key criteria that ensure it supports the overall goals. These standards form the basis for evaluating the quality and effectiveness of execution. To be deemed successful, each task must meet the following vital criteria:

Adherence to the Plan: Every task must be carried out in strict adherence to the strategic approach and methodology detailed in the project plan. This involves carefully following specified procedures, using resources efficiently, and consistently adhering to the established workflow to avoid any deviations from the process. It is crucial to maintain consistent, organized execution to achieve the project's objectives successfully.

Meeting Quality Expectations: To guarantee the project's success, all tasks must meet or exceed the original quality standards. This involves applying thorough quality control, such as detailed inspections and evaluations throughout development. Regular reviews will monitor progress and spot areas for improvement. By addressing issues early, we ensure the final results align with the project's goals and meet stakeholder expectations.

Completion Within the Scheduled Timeframe: Timeliness is essential in project management. To keep the project on track and prevent delays in related tasks, it is critical to complete each task by the set deadlines in the project timeline. Effective time management strategies are key, including using various scheduling tools to carefully monitor progress. This allows project managers to identify potential bottlenecks early, enabling timely interventions and adjustments. Such a proactive approach helps maintain momentum and boosts overall efficiency and productivity.

As the project progresses, various deliverables are created at different stages, each representing an important milestone toward completion. These deliverables—spanning from initial prototypes to final reports—serve vital roles: they guide the project's direction and add value to the overall goal. Every deliverable completed improves the final result, increasing the value for stakeholders and boosting their satisfaction with the project's developments and outcomes.

Successfully managing work involves consistently focusing on details and coordinating efforts across all project components. This includes regular communication among team members, periodic progress reviews, and making adjustments as needed to ensure efforts align with the project's goals. Such oversight helps keep the project on track and ensures it delivers the desired results.

Leading the Team

Execution in any project or initiative relies heavily on leadership. Essentially, good leadership focuses on one core question: How can we motivate and direct our team members to achieve their full potential and perform optimally? During the execution phase, team members depend on the project manager for key elements that support success, such as:

Direction: A clear and well-articulated vision acts as an essential guide for team members, helping them understand their specific roles as well as the project's overall goals. This clarity creates an environment where everyone recognizes how their efforts contribute to the bigger picture, promoting alignment and collaborative progress. By establishing this clear direction, the team can operate more efficiently, reducing misunderstandings and boosting productivity to achieve shared objectives.

Support: Team members need to feel confident that their leader will support them when necessary. This support isn't just about providing resources and information; it also involves fostering an environment with open communication. In such a setting, team members are encouraged to express their concerns and share ideas freely, which builds trust and promotes collaboration. By actively fostering this openness, leaders can establish a foundation that enables their team to succeed.

Problem-solving: In any project, challenges and obstacles are inevitable and often unexpected. A competent leader has the sharp awareness to identify potential problems early, enabling prompt action. They cultivate a workspace where team members are encouraged to participate in open and cooperative dialogue, nurturing teamwork and innovation. By directing these discussions toward positive resolutions, the leader keeps the team focused and motivated, helping to guide the project to success despite setbacks.

Motivation: Maintaining high morale is essential for boosting team productivity. A great leader inspires members by recognizing their individual contributions and celebrating both personal and team successes. This creates a positive environment and strengthens camaraderie among team members. Consequently, this camaraderie boosts their dedication to common goals, propelling the team toward greater achievements.

An effective leader aims to foster a supportive environment where each team member feels valued and understands their specific responsibilities. Balancing encouragement with accountability is key to building a collaborative atmosphere. This approach promotes trust, open communication, and improves overall team performance, enabling the team to function as a united group focused on common objectives.

Communication During Execution

Effective communication is essential during the execution phase of any project. It acts as a key tool to keep all team members aligned and informed as tasks advance. Fundamentally, communication helps answer critical questions like: How can we ensure everyone is on the same page at every stage? During this phase, several important practices should be followed:

Regular Updates: It is essential to share progress updates consistently. This could be in the form of daily stand-ups, weekly reports, or any other format that keeps the team informed about where they stand relative to project milestones. These updates help track progress and identify potential delays early on.

Rapid Issue Communication: Any challenges or obstacles that emerge should be communicated promptly. Addressing issues quickly helps resolve them efficiently, reducing their effect on the project schedule and team morale. This involves fostering a supportive environment where team members feel safe raising problems without fear of repercussions.

Clear Understanding of Changes: Whenever there are modifications to the project scope, timelines, or resource allocation, it's essential to communicate these changes clearly so all stakeholders understand them. Clear communication helps prevent confusion and misalignment, supporting a cohesive approach to new directions.

Effective communication is fundamental to project success. Without proactive communication, carefully planned tasks can deviate from the project's main goals. When all team members share a common understanding and aligned objectives, the chances of success improve greatly, boosting the project's progress with increased efficiency and effectiveness.

Handling Issues and Changes

No project proceeds exactly as planned because of inherent complexities and uncertainties. As projects move forward, issues and unexpected changes are inevitable. This raises an important question: how can we respond effectively when circumstances diverge from our expectations? Common challenges that may emerge during the project include:

Delays in Tasks: Timelines can be affected by unexpected events arising from various sources. These disruptions might stem from reliance on other teams whose deliverables are critical, insufficient allocation of necessary resources, or external circumstances that were not initially considered during the planning phase. Each of these factors can contribute to delays and challenges, ultimately impacting the overall project schedule.

Resource Conflicts: When multiple projects compete for attention, it often leads to conflicting demands for limited resources. This struggle can manifest as personnel shortages, budget constraints, and equipment limitations. Such competition can significantly hinder project progress, creating delays and bottlenecks that impede overall workflow and productivity. As a result, teams may find themselves stretched thin, unable to allocate sufficient focus or manpower to individual initiatives, ultimately jeopardizing project success.

Unexpected Risks: Starting a new project requires awareness that unexpected risks can emerge, which weren't foreseen during planning. These risks may originate from technological advancements that disrupt current workflows, changes in market conditions affecting the project's feasibility, or variations in stakeholder involvement that complicate communication and decisions. Such unpredictable elements can add substantial complexity, demanding quick and effective action to handle them and ensure the project stays on course.

Changes in Requirements: Stakeholder feedback and changing market conditions often lead to updates in project requirements. Managing these changes involves reassessing the project scope to incorporate new demands while still aiming to meet the original objectives. This delicate process requires project managers to balance the advantages of adjustments with their potential effects on schedules, budgets, and overall success.

In light of these challenges, it's imperative for the project manager to respond swiftly and effectively. This includes making necessary adjustments to the project plan and resource allocation while keeping the overall objectives aligned. By remaining adaptable and maintaining clear communication with the team and stakeholders, the project manager can navigate these challenges and steer the project back on course.

Maintaining Alignment with the Plan

Effective project execution should not be interpreted as rigid adherence to the initial plan; rather, it involves implementing the plan while remaining flexible enough to adapt to changing circumstances. A project manager plays a critical role in this process and must ensure that several key elements are consistently monitored and maintained:

Alignment with Scope: It's essential that all work aligns with the project's scope. This includes regularly reviewing project deliverables to ensure they meet predefined objectives and requirements. Any deviations or potential changes should be addressed promptly to prevent scope creep and keep the project focused on its goals.

Adherence to Schedule: The project manager should strive to keep the project on schedule as closely as possible. This requires meticulous planning and continuous monitoring of timelines. Regularly updating the project schedule and communicating any delays or adjustments helps keep the team informed and on track to meet deadlines.

Cost Control: Maintaining control over the project's budget is paramount. The project manager should continuously track expenses and compare them against the budget forecasts. This involves implementing cost management practices to identify potential overruns early and make necessary adjustments to stay within financial constraints.

Quality Standards Maintenance: Upholding established quality standards is critical to the project's success. The project manager must ensure that all deliverables meet the required specifications and that quality assurance processes are actively applied throughout the project lifecycle. Regular quality assessments and feedback loops should be integrated into the workflow to maintain high standards.

Achieving these goals requires the project manager to be highly vigilant and proactive. They must stay closely aware of the project's constantly changing environment, noticing shifts in circumstances and potential issues. This awareness helps them make well-informed, strategic decisions that align with the project's objectives while remaining flexible enough to adapt to new information and challenges. By staying alert and adaptable, the project manager can effectively handle complexities and guide the project to success.

Common Execution Mistakes

Many projects encounter significant obstacles during execution, often due to easily avoidable errors. These common mistakes can greatly impact the efficiency and overall success of a project. When teams neglect planning details, miscommunicate, or miss deadlines, the consequences can affect all parts of the project, risking the achievement of goals and reducing the quality of final deliverables. Proactively addressing these issues is crucial for guiding projects toward successful results. Common mistakes include:

Poor Communication Among Team Members: Effective communication is crucial to any project's success. When team members fail to share information clearly and consistently, misunderstandings and delays can arise, leading to misaligned efforts and wasted resources.

Lack of Leadership or Direction: A project lacking strong leadership can experience guidance shortages, causing team members to feel uncertain about their roles and responsibilities. Effective leadership provides clear direction, which is crucial for aligning everyone toward shared goals with intentionality and synchronization.

Failure to Address Issues Quickly: As projects develop, issues and challenges are unavoidable. If these problems are not dealt with quickly, they can grow into bigger obstacles that threaten the project's timeline and objectives. Acting promptly is essential to keep progress on track.

Ignoring Changes or Risks: The project environment is constantly changing, and unexpected shifts can occur. Ignoring possible risks or not adjusting to new situations may cause major setbacks. Proactively identifying and handling risks is essential for maintaining project progress.

Losing Alignment with the Original Plan: Over time, projects may stray from their original objectives if clarity and focus are lacking. This misalignment can lead the team to pursue different goals that do not support the project's intended outcome.

To avoid these errors, project leaders should promote open communication, maintain a clear vision, and remain adaptable. Recognizing these common pitfalls and taking steps to prevent them can increase the likelihood of successfully completing projects. Additionally, adaptability helps leaders navigate unexpected challenges effectively.

Real-World Example: Executing a House Construction Project

Imagine you are managing the construction of a house, and planning is complete. The design is finalized, the schedule is set, the budget is approved, and the team is ready. Now, work begins.

The foundation is poured, framing begins, and contractors move through each phase of construction. As the project progresses, multiple teams work together, and coordination becomes critical. However, challenges arise. A materials delivery is delayed, shifting the schedule. A contractor identifies an issue requiring rework that affects both time and cost. Weather conditions unexpectedly slow progress.

As the project manager, you must address these challenges while keeping the project on track. This may involve adjusting the schedule, reallocating resources, or communicating changes to stakeholders. At the same time, you must ensure the work meets quality standards and aligns with the original scope. Each decision you make affects the project's overall success. Execution is not about following the plan perfectly. It is about adapting the plan as you move forward.

Connecting to Your Project 2

In Project 2 – The Experience Project, you will begin identifying real-world work experience and translating it into project-based activities. As you embark on this journey, it's essential to start reflecting on the following aspects:

✓ **Did everything go according to plan?** Consider the specific tasks you undertook in your previous roles. What were your responsibilities, and how did you approach them?

✓ **How were issues handled?** Consider how these tasks relate to the project work you are currently involved in. Which skills or experiences from your past can you apply to improve project outcomes?

✓ **What role did communication and leadership play in the outcome?** Reflect on how your execution of these activities is vital to the project's overall success. Every task you complete contributes to the larger goals, so understanding this connection is crucial.

This marks the beginning of integrating project management principles into your experiences, setting the stage for more effective project execution and management in the future.

Closing Thought

Execution is where plans are tested and results are achieved. It is where ideas become reality and leadership truly matters. While planning sets the direction, execution determines success. As you continue your journey, remember that progress is not defined by perfection but by the ability to adapt and move forward.

⚓ *Key Takeaways*

✓ Execution is where the project plan is put into action.

✓ Strong leadership ensures alignment, motivation, and progress.

✓ Communication is essential to coordinate work and resolve issues.

✓ Successful execution depends on preparation during the planning phase.

End-of-Chapter Questions

1. What is the execution phase in project management?
2. What are the primary activities performed during execution?
3. How does execution differ from planning?
4. What role does leadership play during project execution?
5. Why is communication critical during execution?
6. What are deliverables, and how are they produced during execution?
7. What challenges can arise during execution?
8. How can a project manager keep a team aligned during execution?
9. What is the relationship between planning and execution?
10. How does effective execution contribute to overall project success?

📖 *Captain's Log: Discussion Board*

Recall a time when you managed a plan or completed a project. What obstacles did you face, and how did you handle them? Consider how better leadership, communication, and preparation might have enhanced the process and resulted in a more successful outcome.

Chapter 11 – Control Tower Waters
(Monitoring & Controlling)

🎯 *Learning Objectives*

By the end of this chapter, you should be able to:

- ✓ Understand the purpose of monitoring and controlling in project management
- ✓ Identify key performance indicators used to track progress
- ✓ Explain how variance between planned and actual performance is identified
- ✓ Recognize the importance of making timely adjustments
- ✓ Understand how control processes keep projects aligned with objectives

CHAPTER 11

Control Tower Waters

⚓ *Entering Control Tower Waters*

As the Deliverables progresses beyond Execution Bay, activity remains high, but something has changed. The river is now closely monitored, with lookout towers lining the shoreline. Signals are exchanged, observations are recorded, and every movement is tracked precisely.

Captain Brian looks toward the horizon. "We've entered Control Tower Waters," he says.

The crew notices the difference immediately. "Why does everything feel… more controlled?" one crew member asks.

The captain nods. "Because this is where we stop guessing—and start measuring."

He points toward a nearby tower where signals are being sent.

"We're no longer just doing the work. We're making sure the work is being done correctly… and on track."

The crew watches carefully.

"If we drift off course here," the captain continues, "we need to know immediately and correct it before it becomes a bigger problem."

What Is Monitoring and Controlling?

The monitoring and controlling process fundamentally aims to answer: Are we progressing toward our project goals? If not, what corrective actions are needed? This continuous process is crucial to ensuring the project's performance stays in line with the set plan and objectives. Monitoring and controlling involve several key activities, including:

Measuring Progress: This process involves closely monitoring the progress of project tasks and milestones against the established project timeline. By providing regular updates, we can effectively assess the project's progress and determine whether it is proceeding as expected. This ongoing evaluation is crucial for identifying potential delays or obstacles and ensuring that the project remains on track to meet its objectives.

Identifying Variances: Identifying discrepancies between actual and planned project performance is of the highest importance. This involves thoroughly analyzing variations in key areas such as cost, schedule, and scope. By closely examining these deviations, project managers can gain a deeper understanding of their potential impacts and implications for the project's overall success. Understanding the root causes of these discrepancies enables more informed decision-making and effective project adjustments.

Managing Changes: Throughout a project's lifecycle, it is important to understand that changes will happen at different stages. These can result from various factors, including shifting stakeholder expectations, unexpected challenges, or new opportunities. To manage these changes effectively, proactive monitoring and control are essential. This means not only assessing how each change impacts the project's overall performance but also evaluating its effects on timelines, budgets, and resource allocation. By analyzing these impacts carefully, project managers can make informed decisions and make necessary adjustments, helping the project stay aligned with its goals and adapt to changing conditions.

Ensuring Alignment with Project Objectives: Ongoing oversight is essential to ensure the project remains aligned with its objectives throughout its lifecycle. This involves consistently evaluating and reassessing the project's outputs to determine whether they still meet the desired outcomes and satisfy stakeholder expectations. Regular reviews enable adjustments and realignment as needed, fostering a dynamic process that keeps the project on track and responsive to changes in goals or needs.

The monitoring and controlling phase is vital in project management and happens alongside project execution. It involves continuous assessment and oversight throughout the project, enabling real-time evaluation of progress toward goals.

As the project advances, this phase is key for identifying and addressing any deviations from the original plan. Making quick adjustments ensures the project stays aligned with its objectives and timeline, leading to successful completion.

Planned vs. Actual Performance

To properly evaluate a project's progress, it is essential to perform a thorough comparison between the original plans and the current state of the initiative. This detailed review helps answer an important question: Are we on track to reach our expected milestones? By analyzing factors, milestones, and outcomes, we can gain useful insights into how well the project aligns with our initial expectations and identify areas that might need adjustments or more attention. Key areas to focus on for these comparisons include:

Planned Schedule vs. Actual Progress: This involves carefully comparing the project plan's timeline with the milestones achieved to date. By closely tracking task completion against the planned schedule, you can determine whether the project is ahead, behind, or on schedule. This assessment highlights successes and identifies potential delays, enabling timely adjustments to keep the project on track.

Planned Cost vs. Actual Spending: This requires a detailed analysis comparing the estimated budgeted costs with the actual expenses incurred to date. By closely examining the financial data, we can uncover critical insights into the project's financial health. This analysis will allow us to determine whether the project is adhering to its established budgetary constraints, has exceeded its financial limits, or is experiencing unexpected cost savings that could positively impact its overall funding.

Planned Scope vs. Completed Deliverables: This analysis reviews the original project scope, including expected outcomes and deliverables, and compares it with the actual work completed. It offers insights into whether the project remains aligned with its initial goals. The comparison also reveals any changes or deviations during the project's progress, helping stakeholders assess how these modifications might impact the overall success.

By conducting these comparisons, project managers and stakeholders can obtain important insights into the project's progress. This helps determine whether the project is ahead of schedule, behind schedule, or on track to achieve its goals. Such understanding is vital for making informed decisions and taking corrective actions when needed to keep the project on course.

Understanding Variance

Variance is a key metric that reveals the difference between planned objectives and actual results in any project or operation. It measures how much these results deviate from expectations, offering valuable insights into the effectiveness of planning and execution. By analyzing variance, we can better gauge how well our expectations match reality, enabling us to evaluate strategies, make adjustments, and improve performance and outcomes.

This process is crucial for identifying areas needing improvement and ensuring that the project remains on course to meet its objectives. Variance can be divided into specific categories, each focusing on different aspects of project performance. Examples include:

Schedule Variance: This metric measures a project's progress relative to its planned schedule. It offers teams insights into whether important milestones are achieved on time, helping them assess the project's overall status and success. Understanding the pace of progress is essential for identifying potential delays or areas needing attention, helping ensure the project stays on track and meets its objectives.

Cost Variance: This metric assesses whether actual spending matches the original budget. By examining the cost variance, project managers can determine whether they are overspending or underspending against allocated funds. This evaluation is crucial for maintaining strong financial control, ensuring efficient use of resources, and making informed decisions that align with the project's financial objectives. Proper management of cost variance not only helps keep the project on track but also facilitates accountability and foresight in resource allocation.

Minor variances are common and often result from normal fluctuations and adjustments in projects. However, significant or ongoing variances may indicate underlying problems requiring urgent action. For example, repeated schedule delays could indicate resource limitations or unexpected obstacles, while persistent budget overruns might suggest inaccurate estimates or wasteful spending. Quickly addressing these issues is crucial to keeping projects on schedule and aligned with strategic objectives.

Performance Measurement (Introducing Earned Value Concepts)

At its core, performance measurement answers a key question: How well are we executing our plans and objectives? In project management, Earned Value (EV) is one of the most effective tools for measuring performance. It enables project managers to evaluate a project's performance against its baseline plan and assess its financial condition. The main equations compare:

Planned Value (PV): The Planned Value (PV) represents the estimated cost of work scheduled to be completed by a specific milestone in the project timeline. It reflects the project manager's initial estimates of scope and expenses, serving as a key benchmark for performance assessment. By comparing PV with actual costs and progress, stakeholders can evaluate how closely the project adheres to its planned schedule and budget.

Earned Value (EV): Earned Value represents the actual work completed at a given point in the project, compared to the initial budget. It helps project managers see how much of the planned work has been turned into earned revenue or tangible outcomes. This measurement is vital for assessing the project's progress and making informed decisions about future actions.

Actual Cost (AC): Actual Costs refer to the total expenses incurred for work done up to a certain point. This includes all expense types, such as labor costs for personnel, materials purchased and used, and overhead costs like utilities and administrative support. Analyzing AC helps stakeholders assess the project's financial health by comparing actual spending against the budget and determining whether it is progressing as planned.

By comparing the three key metrics: Planned Value (PV), Earned Value (EV), and Actual Cost (AC), project managers can assess the project's overall health. This comparison helps determine whether the project is on schedule and within budget. It also identifies variances that may require corrective actions to resolve performance issues, ensuring the project's successful and efficient delivery on schedule and within budget.

Earned Value Formula Visual

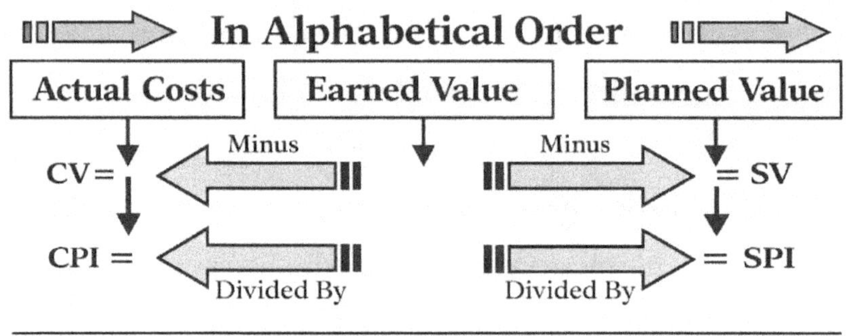

EV Formula:

$$CV = EV - AC \qquad EV - PV = SV$$

$$CPI = EV / AC \qquad EV / PV = SPI$$

Managing Changes

No project proceeds exactly as initially planned. Change is an essential part of the project lifecycle. Central to successful project management is change management, which addresses a key question: How can we manage changes effectively while keeping all stakeholders and project goals aligned? Changes may arise in various forms, including:

Scope Adjustments: This process involves adjusting the specific outcomes or deliverables of the project. It may include expanding or narrowing the project's objectives based on new requirements, important stakeholder feedback, or changes in market conditions. These modifications are essential to ensure the project remains relevant and aligned with the evolving needs of the organization and its target audience.

Schedule Shifts: Adjustments to project timelines happen regularly due to unexpected delays, resource availability, or the need for more time to finish key tasks properly. These changes can result from unforeseen events disrupting the workflow, changes in project priorities, or the complexity of specific activities that demand extra effort to guarantee quality results.

Cost Updates: Projects often require budget adjustments due to unexpected expenses from scope changes or updates in resource costs. Reassessments of funding needs can also lead to further budget modifications. These dynamics can greatly influence the project's financial planning and execution.

Resource Reallocation: This process entails thoroughly reviewing and reallocating human, technological, or material resources allocated to the project. The aim is to ensure that the right skills and tools are available at the right times, promoting smooth and efficient project execution. This might involve identifying personnel with specialized expertise, upgrading or integrating new technologies, and making sure essential materials are on hand to meet evolving project needs.

Effective change management doesn't aim to prevent all changes, which is unrealistic. Instead, it focuses on managing change in a controlled and organized way. This includes establishing a systematic process to evaluate and approve changes, keeping all stakeholders informed, and maintaining the project's integrity.

Uncontrolled or poorly managed changes can result in several issues, including scope creep, where the project's scope expands without proper oversight, leading to delays and budget overruns. Moreover, unmanaged changes can destabilize team cohesion and cause misaligned expectations among team members and stakeholders, making project execution more difficult. By prioritizing effective change management, project managers can minimize risks, improve project alignment, and ultimately achieve successful project outcomes.

Taking Corrective Action

When performance issues occur in a project, it is crucial to respond quickly and effectively to minimize their impact on overall progress. Handling these problems requires a careful assessment of the situation, focusing on the key question: How can we adjust our efforts to achieve our goals? Taking corrective steps means implementing specific strategies to overcome current setbacks and realign the project for success. This can involve a variety of methods, such as:

Adjusting the Schedule: This process involves reviewing the project timeline to manage delays or changes in expected deliverables. It may include extending deadlines for certain tasks to improve completion rates or reorganizing the sequence of activities. This restructuring is designed to help us meet our key milestones on time, even if we need to make adjustments during the process.

Reallocating Resources: This process typically involves a thorough examination of how personnel, tools, and budgetary resources are currently allocated. By strategically reallocating these resources, such as assigning additional team members to departments or tasks facing delays, or redirecting financial resources toward high-priority projects, organizations can significantly improve their operational efficiency. This careful realignment not only alleviates bottlenecks but also revitalizes the project's overall momentum, ensuring it remains on track for successful completion.

Addressing Risks: Taking a proactive stance on risk management is vital for project success. This means not only identifying new risks arising from performance issues but also revisiting previously identified risks. It's crucial to evaluate if these risks have changed in their scope or impact, as this can influence the project's progress. After thoroughly analyzing potential risks, teams should develop and apply effective mitigation strategies to minimize their effects on the overall project. This approach helps teams protect their goals and increases the chances of success.

Revising Plans: This process involves thoroughly reviewing the initial project plans and making needed modifications to match current conditions. This could include adjusting the project scope, updating deliverable specifications to meet current demands, or realigning stakeholder expectations with the present reality. Each change is intended to develop a more practical and attainable project framework capable of addressing challenges that have emerged since the project's start.

The main goal of these corrective actions is to minimize the impact of deviations from the original plan, helping the project stay aligned with its overall objectives. Using a variety of strategies, project teams can work together to manage and overcome challenges effectively. This proactive approach not only resolves issues promptly but also keeps the project on track for success, promoting a collective effort to reach the intended goals.

Common Monitoring & Controlling Mistakes

Projects frequently encounter major challenges when diligent performance tracking is overlooked. Without proper monitoring, delays and problems can occur that could have been prevented through careful oversight and proactive management. Ignoring performance metrics can lead teams to face unforeseen issues that slow their progress and affect their overall success. Here are several common mistakes that project teams tend to make:

Infrequent Progress Tracking: Many teams struggle to establish a regular routine for assessing their progress toward goals. Without consistent check-ins, identifying early signs of problems becomes harder. Consequently, issues may develop unnoticed and escalate, causing bigger setbacks that could have been prevented with earlier intervention. The lack of frequent evaluations not only hampers the team's ability to stay on course but also reduces their overall efficiency.

Neglecting Minor Variances: Teams often overlook minor performance differences, dismissing them as insignificant. Yet, these small variances can accumulate over time, leading to major problems if ignored. What starts as a simple mistake can escalate, complicating project management and causing a ripple effect that reduces overall efficiency. Detecting and correcting these subtle issues early is essential to preserving project integrity and enabling smooth progress.

Lack of Comparison to Initial Plans: Regularly comparing actual performance metrics with the original project plan is crucial for project success. This constant review helps teams stay aligned with their goals and objectives. Without it, they might miss deviations from the plan, which could cause serious problems that are hard to fix later. Monitoring these metrics closely allows teams to quickly spot discrepancies and adjust as needed, keeping them on course to reach their desired results.

Poor Change Management Practices: When unforeseen changes occur in a project, teams often lack a clear framework to manage them. This gap in change management can cause confusion among team members, leading to miscommunication and unclear roles. As the project progresses, these issues can accumulate and threaten to derail progress, jeopardizing the project's success and weakening team unity. Therefore, adopting a structured change management approach is essential to address these issues effectively.

Delay in Corrective Actions: Once problems are identified, some teams often hesitate to act swiftly and implement corrective actions. This delay can cause the issues to worsen, making resolution more difficult and increasing future costs. Procrastinating on these challenges can turn what was initially manageable into a more complicated and costly situation.

To greatly improve the chances of project success, it is essential to cultivate a strong sense of discipline within the team and implement regular monitoring practices. This proactive approach helps identify and resolve potential issues early and ensures the project stays aligned with its overall goals throughout its lifecycle. By adopting these practices, teams can stay focused, respond quickly to changes, and ultimately ensure projects are successfully completed.

Real-World Example: Monitoring a House Construction Project

Imagine you are managing the construction of a house, and work is underway. You have a plan in place, but now you must ensure the project stays on track. As construction progresses, you compare actual progress to your schedule. You notice that framing is taking longer than expected, which could delay subsequent tasks such as electrical and plumbing work. This creates a schedule variance that must be addressed.

At the same time, you review your budget and find that material costs are higher than expected. This creates a cost variance that could affect the overall budget if not managed carefully. To address these issues, you may need to take corrective action. This could include reallocating resources to accelerate framing or identifying cost-saving opportunities in other areas of the project.

You also monitor quality and ensure all work meets required standards. If issues are identified, they must be corrected immediately to prevent further delays and additional costs. By continuously monitoring performance and making adjustments, you can keep the project aligned with its objectives and avoid major disruptions.

Connecting to Your Project 2

At this stage, you are actively thinking about how work is tracked and evaluated in real-world scenarios. For Project 2 – The Experience Project, consider:

- How performance was measured in your past work

- How progress was tracked and reported

- How issues or changes were handled

Understanding these elements will help you translate your experience into project-based language.

Reflection Questions

Think about a time when a project or task began to go off track. How was the issue identified? Was action taken promptly, or did the problem grow over time? What could have been done to detect and correct the issue earlier?

Closing Thought

Execution advances a project, while monitoring and controlling ensure it stays on track. Without measurement, progress is uncertain. By tracking performance, spotting variances, and making adjustments, you preserve control over the project's course. Keep in mind that success isn't just about completing tasks, but about making sure those tasks result in the intended outcomes.

⚓ *Key Takeaways*

- ✓ Monitoring and controlling ensure the project stays on track
- ✓ Performance is measured against the project plan
- ✓ Variances help identify gaps between expected and actual results
- ✓ Timely corrective actions prevent small issues from becoming major problems
- ✓ Continuous oversight improves the likelihood of project success

End-of-Chapter Questions

1. What is the purpose of the monitoring and controlling phase?

2. What are key performance indicators (KPIs) in project management?

3. What is a variance in a project?

4. Why is it important to compare actual performance to the plan?

5. What types of issues can be identified through monitoring?

6. What is corrective action in project management?

7. How can delays or cost overruns be managed?

8. Why is continuous oversight important during a project?

9. How does monitoring support decision-making?

10. How does effective control contribute to project success?

Captain's Log: Discussion Board

Recall a moment when you needed to change your approach during a task or project. What signs indicated things were going wrong, and how did you respond? Consider how regularly checking progress and making prompt adjustments can enhance results and ensure your efforts stay aligned with the initial plan.

Chapter 12 – Leadership Lookout

(Leadership Principles)

⌖ *Learning Objectives*

By the end of this chapter, you should be able to:

- ✓ Understand the difference between managing projects and leading people
- ✓ Identify key leadership qualities that contribute to project success
- ✓ Explain the role of emotional intelligence in leadership
- ✓ Recognize how leadership styles influence team performance
- ✓ Understand how effective leadership builds trust, alignment, and accountability

CHAPTER 12

Leadership Lookout

⚓ *Entering Leadership Lookout*

As the *Deliverables* moves beyond Control Tower Waters, the river begins to rise toward higher ground. A lookout spire rises ahead, offering a view of the entire journey, from the calm start to the challenging rapids.

Captain Brian steps away from the wheel and walks toward the tower. "We've arrived at Leadership Lookout," he says.

The crew follows after him. From the Lookout, they have a clear view of everything, their journey so far, and the waters ahead.

"Why are we stopping here?" one crew member asks.

The captain looks out across the horizon. "Because this is where you stop managing tasks… and start leading people."

The crew grows quiet.

"A plan can guide the journey," he continues, "but leadership determines whether the team makes it together."

Leadership in Project Management

Effective leadership revolves around a key question: How can we lead individuals and teams to reach a common goal? In project management, leadership goes beyond just holding authority; it involves influence, trust, and accountability. While project planning provides the structure and details of tasks, leadership primarily influences how well those tasks are carried out. Project managers have several essential responsibilities that are vital for creating a successful team environment:

Aligning Teams Toward a Common Objective: To create a harmonious work environment, project managers should communicate a clear vision and set shared goals. This alignment is essential because it directs everyone's efforts toward common objectives, reducing misunderstandings and confusion. As a result, it leads to a more efficient and productive team. When each person understands their role within the bigger picture, it improves collaboration and increases the overall effectiveness in reaching project goals.

Building Trust and Accountability: Trust is the essential base for successful teamwork. Project managers are key in creating an environment where all team members feel valued and respected. This supportive setting promotes open communication, enabling team members to share their ideas, concerns, and feedback with confidence, thereby improving collaboration.

In contrast, accountability involves establishing clear expectations for each team member and consistently following up on their tasks and responsibilities. This approach empowers individuals to take ownership of their roles, boosting their sense of responsibility and reinforcing commitment to team goals. The blend of trust and accountability fosters a strong synergy that propels the team's success.

Navigating Conflict and Uncertainty: In any project, challenges and disagreements are inevitable, often stemming from differing opinions or unexpected obstacles. A strong leader can address these conflicts head-on, leading the team toward constructive discussions to achieve a resolution. This requires listening to diverse perspectives and fostering open communication. Moreover, project managers are essential in handling uncertainties that could jeopardize the project's progress. They need to stay flexible, modifying plans as needed, while keeping the team focused, motivated, and united. In this way, strong leaders can transform conflicts into chances for development and progress.

Motivating People with Different Goals and Views: Team members often bring diverse backgrounds, experiences, and values that can significantly impact their input. A proficient project manager recognizes these differences and actively leverages them to foster a more innovative and energetic team environment. This involves exploring each person's unique motivations, understanding what influences them, and connecting their individual goals to the project's main objectives. Doing so not only boosts collaboration but also makes sure each team member feels appreciated, involved, and motivated to contribute to the project's success.

By demonstrating effective leadership qualities, project managers create an environment where teams are motivated to succeed and reach their full potential. Good leadership does more than steer projects to their goals; it promotes a culture of teamwork, open dialogue, and ongoing growth. This encouraging setting not only helps achieve project objectives but also supports team members' personal development. In the end, it establishes a foundation for personal satisfaction and team success, resulting in a vibrant workplace where everyone can excel.

Organizational Structures and Leadership

The structure of an organization deeply influences its leadership environment. It defines how authority is allocated and decision-making is centralized, which in turn affects leadership dynamics. This relationship directly impacts both leadership effectiveness and the organization's overall performance. Clear roles and responsibilities, shaped by these structures, enhance communication and teamwork, creating a supportive environment where leadership can flourish and guide the organization toward its objectives.

At its core, organizational structure explores how authority is assigned within the organization. This allocation of power greatly affects interactions between leaders and teams, influencing communication, collaboration, and project decision-making. The structure outlines responsibilities and also affects the organizational culture, shaping how decisions are made and implemented at various levels.

Common Organizational Structures:

Functional Organizations

In functional organizations, teams are organized by specialty, such as marketing, finance, human resources, and production. Each department functions independently, concentrating on its specific domain. In such structures, project managers generally have limited authority and depend heavily on functional managers for resources and support. Leadership is usually indirect; project managers must coordinate through different departmental heads to reach their objectives. This setup can sometimes lead to slower decision-making and more complicated communication between departments.

Matrix Organizations (Weak, Balanced, Strong)

Matrix organizations feature a dual authority system that combines functional and project-based management. In this environment, authority is shared between functional managers and project managers, creating a more complex leadership dynamic.

In **Weak Matrix Organizations**, Authority mainly lies with functional managers, which often restricts project managers' influence and control. As a result, project managers face challenges in resource allocation and decision-making, and must rely on functional managers' approval and cooperation to meet project goals. They must navigate a complex hierarchy and collaboration process.

Balanced Matrix Organizations seek to balance the distribution of authority, allowing project managers some control over their projects while collaborating closely with functional leaders. This setup encourages shared decision-making, letting both project managers and functional heads contribute their expertise. Consequently, teams can utilize diverse skills and perspectives, resulting in more innovative solutions and better project results.

In **Strong Matrix Organizations**, Project managers hold a higher level of authority and independence, enabling them to manage their projects with control akin to that in projectized organizations. They are not just task coordinators; they are responsible for making crucial decisions and guiding the project's direction. Meanwhile, they keep essential ties to functional areas to promote collaboration and coordination across departments. This balance helps them effectively utilize resources while managing organizational complexities.

Effective leadership in matrix organizations hinges on strong collaboration skills. Project managers face the complex task of negotiating resource allocation, which involves balancing the priorities across various departments. This demands a clear understanding of project objectives and the skill to prioritize tasks amid competing demands, making sure all stakeholders feel heard and their needs are met. By using effective negotiation and communication, leaders can create a collaborative environment that boosts productivity and supports project success.

Projectized Organizations

In projectized organizations, the structure centers on projects instead of functions. Project managers hold complete authority over resources, budgets, and decision-making, enabling faster decisions and sharper focus on project goals. They are empowered to lead teams directly, establish project-specific roles, and allocate resources as required. As a result, leadership in such environments is more direct and outcome-focused, promoting a culture of accountability and quick response.

Understanding organizational structures helps project managers adapt their leadership, manage authority, and improve stakeholder communication, increasing project success in different organizational environments.

Leadership Theories

The concept of leadership has been extensively researched, leading to numerous foundational theories. Each offers valuable insights into human motivation and behavior. Analyzing these theories enhances our understanding of how leaders influence individuals and how effective leadership can inspire and unify teams toward common objectives.

Leadership Theories we will cover

✓ **Maslow's Hierarchy of Entrepreneurial Needs:** What motivates individuals at different stages of growth?

✓ **McGregor's Theory X and Theory Y:** How do leaders view and manage their teams?

✓ **McClelland's Needs Theory:** What drives individual behavior in the workplace?

✓ **Ethics in Leadership:** How should leaders make decisions?

✓ **Conscious Leadership:** How do leaders align purpose with action?

✓ **Symbiotic Leadership:** How do individuals and teams grow and succeed together?

Maslow's Hierarchy of Entrepreneurial Needs

Essentially, this model explores what motivates individuals as they move through various stages of personal and professional development. Maslow's hierarchy offers a framework for understanding these motivations, outlining a progression through several specific levels of need:

✓ **Basic Needs:** At the core are basic survival needs, like sufficient income and stability. These must be fulfilled first, allowing individuals to then pursue higher levels of motivation.

✓ **Security and Sustainability:** After fulfilling their basic needs, people look for security, both financial and emotional, as well as consistency in their lives and careers, along with the ability to plan ahead.

✓ **Relationships and Belonging:** As individuals progress, maintaining social connections becomes increasingly crucial. This stage highlights the importance of cultivating relationships and fostering a sense of belonging within a community or team.

✓ **Recognition and Achievement:** Once a sense of belonging is established, individuals commonly seek recognition for their efforts and achievements. This encompasses professional awards, personal milestones, and approval from peers.

✓ **Purpose and Legacy:** Finally, at the highest level, individuals seek a sense of purpose. They are motivated by the desire to leave a meaningful legacy and contribute positively to the world around them.

As people go through different stages of growth, their motivations change accordingly. Effective leaders understand each team member's place in this process. By recognizing and understanding these various development phases, leaders can align opportunities and offer support tailored to each individual's needs. This deliberate approach promotes personal growth and helps team members succeed on their unique journeys, resulting in a more cohesive and productive team.

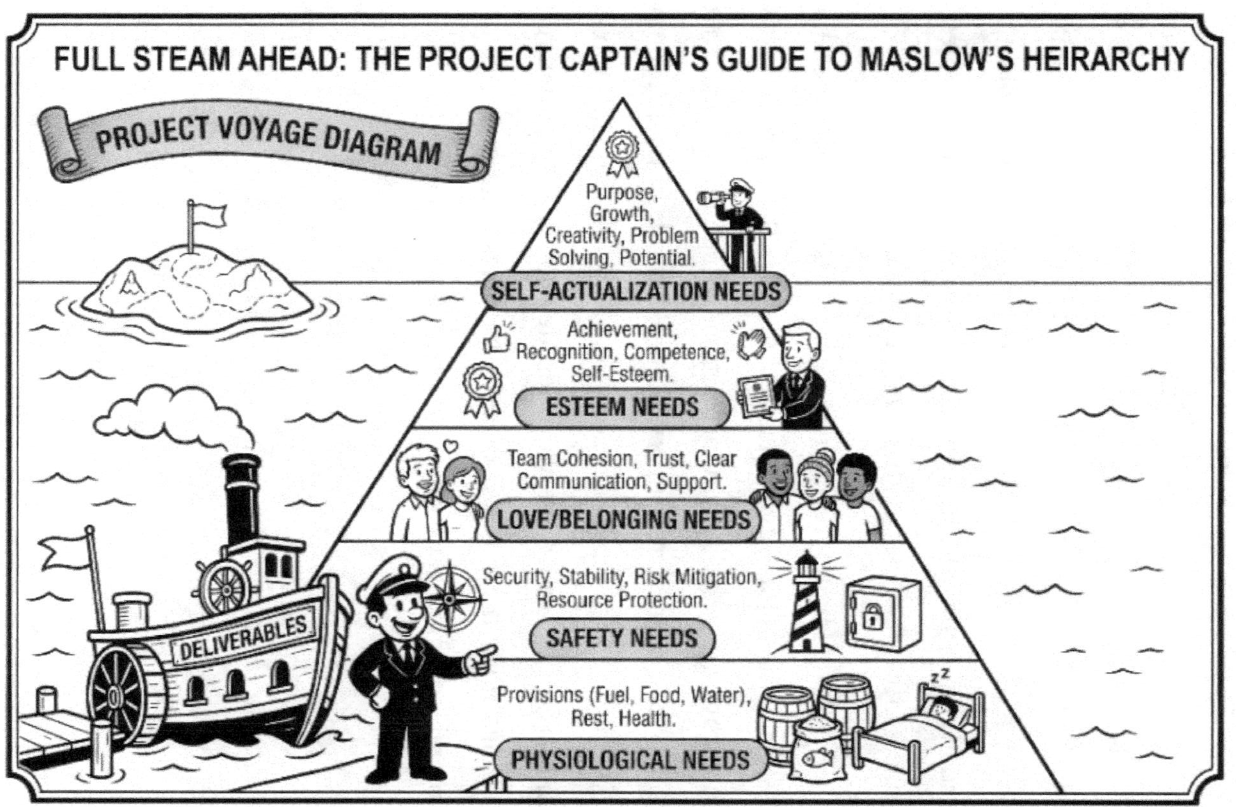

FULL STEAM AHEAD: THE PROJECT CAPTAIN'S GUIDE TO MASLOW'S HEIRARCHY
PROJECT VOYAGE DIAGRAM
Purpose, Growth, Creativity, Problem Solving, Potential.
SELF-ACTUALIZATION NEEDS
Achievement, Recognition, Competence, Self-Esteem.
ESTEEM NEEDS
Team Cohesion, Trust, Clear Communication, Support.
LOVE/BELONGING NEEDS
Security, Stability, Risk Mitigation, Resource Protection.
SAFETY NEEDS
Provisions (Fuel, Food, Water), Rest, Health.
PHYSIOLOGICAL NEEDS
DELIVERABLES

McGregor's Theory X and Theory Y

This theory examines how leaders perceive and manage their teams differently. It considers a key question: How do leaders see their team members, and how do these views shape their leadership style and team interactions? McGregor's division of leadership styles into two categories highlights the underlying beliefs behind managerial actions and how these beliefs affect team motivation and performance.

With **Theory X,** Leaders believe that people generally dislike work and will avoid it unless they are closely supervised and provided with detailed instructions. This view implies that employees need strict supervision, clear rules, and ongoing motivation from management. As a result, organizations embracing a Theory X style often develop highly structured settings with rigid rules, clear hierarchies, and a focus on compliance. Such environments can create a more inflexible workplace culture that might hinder creativity and lower employee morale.

In contrast, **Theory Y** presents a more optimistic perspective, proposing that people are inherently self-motivated, eager for responsibility, and capable of self-management. Leaders endorsing Theory Y believe that with proper conditions and a supportive environment, employees will be motivated to give their best. This approach fosters a work environment centered on trust, independence, and collaboration. In Theory Y organizations, leaders tend to emphasize empowering employees, fostering innovation, and supporting open communication, which can result in increased job satisfaction and productivity.

Choosing between Theory X and Theory Y significantly influences organizational culture and team management. This decision directly affects employee engagement and interpersonal interactions within the workplace. Ultimately, choosing the right management style is essential for influencing team interactions and creating a positive, productive workplace.

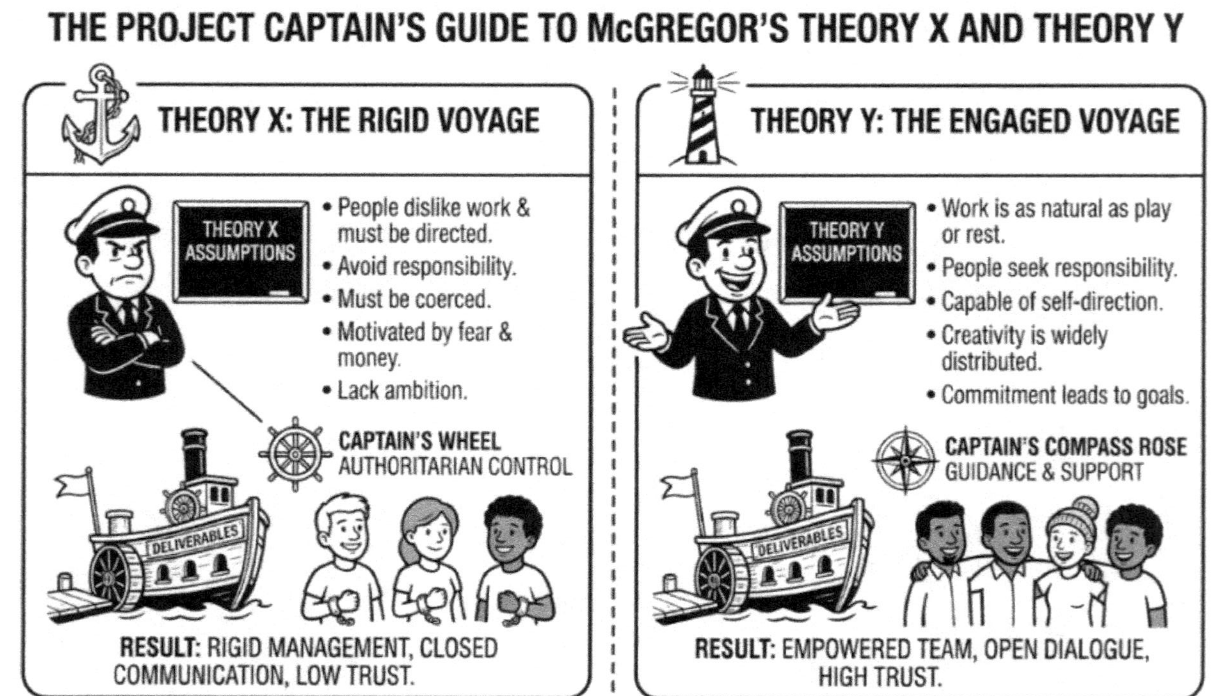
THE PROJECT CAPTAIN'S GUIDE TO McGREGOR'S THEORY X AND THEORY Y
THEORY X: THE RIGID VOYAGE
THEORY X ASSUMPTIONS
People dislike work & must be directed.
Avoid responsibility.
Must be coerced.
Motivated by fear & money.
Lack ambition.
CAPTAIN'S WHEEL
AUTHORITARIAN CONTROL
DELIVERABLES
RESULT: RIGID MANAGEMENT, CLOSED COMMUNICATION, LOW TRUST.
THEORY Y: THE ENGAGED VOYAGE
THEORY Y ASSUMPTIONS
Work is as natural as play or rest.
People seek responsibility.
Capable of self-direction.
Creativity is widely distributed.
Commitment leads to goals.
CAPTAIN'S COMPASS ROSE
GUIDANCE & SUPPORT
DELIVERABLES
RESULT: EMPOWERED TEAM, OPEN DIALOGUE, HIGH TRUST.

McClelland's Needs Theory

This model aims to explore the various factors that influence individual behavior in a work setting. It examines how elements such as personal values, workplace culture, colleagues' relationships, and organizational policies interact to shape employees' actions and decisions. It highlights three main motivators that influence employees:

Achievement: This motivator represents a person's natural drive to set, pursue, and ultimately achieve specific goals. Those motivated by achievement tend to seek opportunities that test their abilities and allow them to showcase their competence and skills. They take pride in their successes and are fueled by the desire for excellence, aiming for both personal and professional development.

Affiliation: This describes a person's desire for social interaction, relationships, and a sense of belonging to a group or organization. People motivated by affiliation prioritize teamwork, collaboration, and supportive relationships with colleagues. They perform best in settings that foster camaraderie and mutual support, and their productivity tends to rise when they feel a strong emotional connection to their team.

Power: This motivator reflects the desire to influence, lead, and make an impact on others. Power-driven individuals seek roles that allow them to exercise authority and participate in decision-making. They are often motivated by the opportunity to shape results and inspire those around them, whether through formal leadership roles or informal influence within a team.

Understanding that different individuals are motivated by these needs to different extents is key to effective leadership. Leaders should tailor their strategies to support and motivate team members based on their specific drivers, thereby creating a more productive and harmonious work environment.

THE PROJECT CAPTAIN'S GUIDE TO McCLELLAND'S NEEDS THEORY
[cite: 1.1, 1.3]
FULL STEAM AHEAD
NEED FOR ACHIEVEMENT (nAch)
SETTING HIGH GOALS & OVERCOMING OBSTACLES [cite: 1.1]
MILESTONE ISLAND
DELIVERABLES
• Seeking calculated risk-taking for difficult goals.
• Wanting regular feedback to track progress. [cite: 1.1]
• A desire to accomplish something through self-effort.
• Finding personal satisfaction in mastering difficult tasks.
PROBLEMS
OPPORTUNITIES,
FEEDBACK PROVIDED
RESULT: FOCUS ON METRICS, CONTINUOUS IMPROVEMENT, HIGH ACHIEVEMENT. [cite: 1.1]
NEED FOR AFFILIATION (nAff)
BUILDING SUPPORTIVE TEAMS & POSITIVE RELATIONSHIPS [cite: 1.1]
• Desiring acceptance and being part of a group. [cite: 1.1]
• Finding comfort in cooperative team environments. [cite: 1.1]
• Avoiding conflict and creating a harmonous atmosphere.
• Concern for maintaining interpersonal relationships. [cite: 1.1]
TEAM COHESION.
RESULT: TEAM COLLABORATION, LOW STRESS, COMMUNICATION. [cite: 1.1]
NEED FOR POWER (nPow)
INFLUENCING OTHERS & HAVING IMPACT ON OUTCOMES [cite: 1.1]
POWER & CONTROL
• Desiring to coach, teach, and direct others. (PERSONAL POWER)
• Seeking positions of status and prestige.
• Influencing group members to adopt one's point of view. (INSTITUTIONAL POWER)
• Wanting to be in charge and make decisions.
DELIVERABLES
DECISION AUTHORITY
PROJECT HIERARCHY
RESULT: LEADERSHIP POSITIONS, ORGANIZATIONAL POWER, VISION. [cite: 1.1]

Ethics in Leadership

Essentially, ethics offers guidance to leaders on decision-making, focusing on the moral aspects of their choices and actions. Ethical leadership is characterized by several key principles:

Integrity: Leaders demonstrate honesty and consistency in their values, actions, and words, emphasizing the importance of doing what is right regardless of the situation or potential outcomes.

Fairness: Ethical leaders aim to advance justice and fairness by treating all stakeholders with respect and consideration, while avoiding favoritism or discrimination in their decisions.

Transparency: Open communication and clarity are essential elements of ethical leadership. Leaders need to be transparent about their decisions, explain the reasoning, and discuss potential impacts, which helps build trust and encourages open dialogue.

Accountability: The core of an Ethical Leader is assuming responsibility for their actions and decisions. They recognize their mistakes, learn from them, and are prepared to be accountable to their teams and stakeholders.

In project management, ethical decision-making is essential. Acting with integrity and fairness fosters trust and teamwork, which are critical for successful team collaboration. Upholding a reputation founded on ethical standards promotes long-term success by increasing the credibility of leaders and their organizations among clients, employees, and the broader community. Ethical leadership is more than just adhering to principles; it encompasses cultivating a culture that values and maintains ethical behavior at every level.

THE PROJECT CAPTAIN'S GUIDE TO ETHICS IN LEADERSHIP

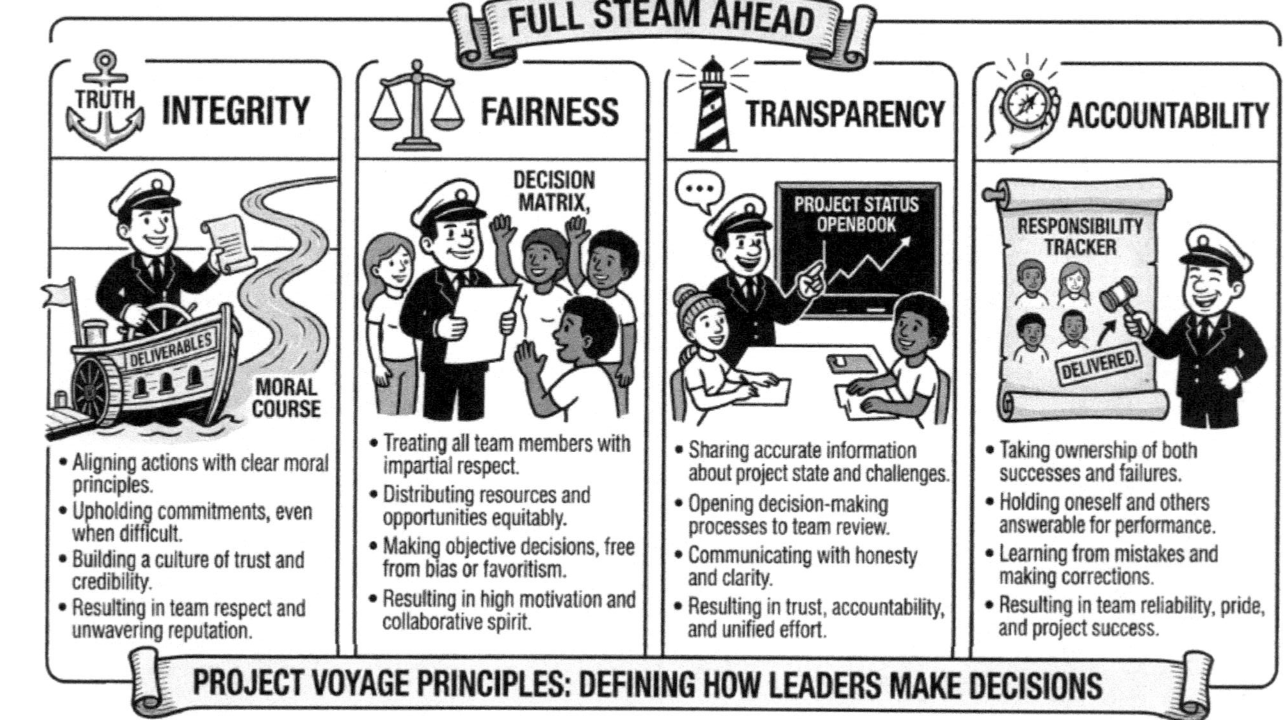

Conscious Leadership

Fundamentally, this model aims to answer a key question: How can leaders successfully align their organization's purpose with practical actions? Conscious leadership is built upon several core principles that guide this alignment:

Purpose-Driven Work: Conscious leaders must ensure that every initiative and project is rooted in a clear, compelling purpose. This requires articulating a vision that inspires and motivates all team members, fostering a sense of meaning and commitment to their work.

Stakeholder Alignment: Conscious leaders must engage and align diverse stakeholders, including employees, customers, investors, and the community. This coordination fosters a unified approach to reaching goals by incorporating a range of perspectives and interests into decision-making.

Authenticity and Trust: Conscious leaders focus on building genuine relationships within their organizations. Through transparency, consistency, and sincerity in their communication and actions, they foster a culture of trust that encourages team members to be open, honest, and innovative.

Long-Term Impact: Conscious leadership prioritizes long-term impacts over immediate gains, highlighting the importance of considering how decisions affect all stakeholders and the environment. This proactive perspective promotes sustainable practices that support both the organization and society at large.

Ultimately, Conscious leaders realize that success depends not only on outcomes but also on the integrity of the processes behind them. By promoting a culture that upholds these principles, they establish a foundation for authentic leadership that strongly influences their organizations and extends beyond them.

Limitations of Traditional Leadership Theories

Each leadership theory provides important insights into team dynamics and organizational success, particularly in project management, but none completely encapsulate the complexities of modern project team environments. Several common gaps can be identified in these theories:

Focus on Individual Motivation: While many theories highlight the significance of individual drivers and motivations, they often neglect the crucial role of team interdependence. In practice, a project's success heavily depends on how effectively team members work together and support each other toward shared objectives.

Leadership Principles: Traditional methods often depict leadership as a one-way process, with leaders giving direction and team members following. This perspective overlooks the relational nature of leadership, which is crucial for building a culture of collaboration, trust, and open communication within teams.

Performance vs. Relationships: Performance metrics are often treated separately from the underlying relationships that shape team dynamics. Focusing only on results may overlook how interpersonal connections influence success. In fact, strong relationships can boost performance by improving communication and creating a supportive workplace.

Mutual Accountability Framework: Teams often lack a formal framework for mutual accountability. Without well-defined processes for shared responsibility, members might find it difficult to hold one another accountable, potentially hindering progress and affecting team cohesion.

In real-world projects, success depends not only on individual motivation or leadership styles but primarily on how well team members collaborate and align their efforts to reach common goals. Key elements include strong teamwork, transparent communication, and a common purpose, all of which are essential for handling the complexities of modern projects.

THE PROJECT CAPTAIN'S GUIDE TO CONSCIOUS LEADERSHIP
FULL STEAM AHEAD

ALIGNING PURPOSE WITH ACTION
PURPOSE
Vision
DELIVERABLES
• Connecting daily tasks to a larger mission.
• Inspiring team commitment through shared values.
• Making value-based decisions in project choices.
• Result: A motivated crew with a clear destination.

HARMONIZING INTERESTS
Partnership
EMPLOYEES
COMMUNITY
CUSTOMERS
EMPLOYEES
• Considering the needs of all project stakeholders.
• Fostering shared understanding and collaboration.
• Resolving conflicts to find win-win solutions.
• Result: Enhanced project support and reputation.

LEADERSHIP BY EXAMPLE
integrity
• Acting with consistency and transparency.
• Admitting mistakes and seeking feedback.
• Empowering the team to build mutual respect.
• Result: A high-trust team ready for challenges.

CREATING SUSTAINABLE VALUE
Sustainability
VOYAGE BEYOND
DELIVERABLES
• Making decisions for future sustainability.
• Building lasting systems and project value.
• Mentoring future leaders for continuous growth.
• Result: Projects that benefit society and people.

PROJECT VOYAGE PRINCIPLES: DEFINING HOW LEADERS MAKE DECISIONS

Introducing Symbiotic Leadership

In the book, **"Symbiosis: Utilizing Symbiotic Leadership to Guide and Improve Relationships,"** the concept of Symbiotic Leadership explores a different question: How can individuals and teams work together effectively to develop and succeed? It extends traditional theories by addressing their limitations. Unlike earlier models that mainly concentrate on motivation, authority, or individual actions, Symbiotic Leadership emphasizes the interdependent relationship between people and performance. It understands that lasting success results not from isolated efforts but from aligned and mutually beneficial collaboration.

Mutual Growth: Success Is Shared

Mutual growth answers: How do individuals develop while contributing to team success? Conventional leadership models often emphasize personal accomplishments, such as hitting targets, finishing tasks, or pursuing individual goals. Although these results are valuable, they may inadvertently foster environments where people focus more on personal gains than on team success.

Symbiotic Leadership shifts this perspective by emphasizing that individual growth and team success are interconnected. When team members develop new skills, gain confidence, and expand their capabilities, the team's overall performance improves. At the same time, when the team succeeds, individuals benefit from recognition, experience, and opportunity. In project management, this means leaders actively look for ways to:

- Develop team members while completing project work

- Assign tasks that both deliver results and build capability

- Encourage knowledge sharing across the team

The result is a team that not only completes the project but also becomes stronger and more capable through the experience.

Reciprocal Accountability: Leaders and Teams Support Each Other

Reciprocal accountability addresses the question: How can we foster shared responsibility for success? In many conventional settings, accountability typically flows one way, from leaders to their teams. Leaders delegate tasks, oversee progress, and hold individuals accountable for outcomes. Although this approach provides control, it may also reduce engagement and personal ownership.

Symbiotic Leadership presents a two-way accountability model. Leaders are responsible for providing direction, support, and clarity, while team members are responsible for delivering results, communicating challenges, and contributing to the team's success.

This creates a balanced relationship where:

- ✓ Leaders are accountable to their teams for support and guidance
- ✓ Team members are accountable for performance and communication
- ✓ Success and failure are shared, not assigned

In practice, this means creating an environment where:

- ✓ Team members feel comfortable raising issues early
- ✓ Leaders actively remove obstacles and provide support
- ✓ Accountability is seen as a shared commitment, not a form of control

This approach builds trust among all participants and encourages a shared sense of ownership within the project. Involving individuals at every level empowers them to take initiative and responsibility. This, in turn, fosters a collaborative environment where everyone feels valued and engaged in the process.

Relational Alignment: Strong Relationships Drive Performance

Relational alignment fundamentally highlights how interpersonal dynamics greatly influence the success of any work or project. While many modern leadership models treat relationships as secondary and prioritize performance and results, Symbiotic Leadership disputes this, arguing that strong relationships are a core driver of performance rather than just an outcome. Strong and well-established relationships within a team or organization lead to several key benefits:

Enhanced Communication: Team members tend to participate more actively in open dialogue, exchange ideas freely, and offer constructive feedback. This boost in communication fosters a more collaborative setting in which all feel appreciated and heard.

Effective Conflict Resolution: Strong relationships build a foundation of trust, encouraging team members to be open to understanding each other's perspectives. This openness helps resolve conflicts more efficiently and constructively, reducing drama and misunderstandings.

Natural Collaboration: Teams that have strong relational ties usually collaborate more smoothly. Members cooperate more harmoniously, leveraging each other's strengths and skills, which results in innovative solutions and higher overall productivity.

Trust and Reduced Friction: Trust acts as a lubricant in decision-making processes. When team members trust each other, it reduces friction and hesitation, leading to faster, more effective decisions.

On the other hand, weak relationships can lead to significant problems such as misalignment, misunderstandings, and operational inefficiencies, despite well-defined processes. These weaknesses often manifest as ineffective team interactions, hesitation to provide feedback, and a tendency to avoid conflicts.

Relational alignment is focused on cultivating and maintaining strong interpersonal relationships by ensuring that:

Understanding of Roles and Perspectives: Team members develop a detailed, intricate understanding of one another's roles, responsibilities, and perspectives. This clarity promotes empathy, enabling team members to better appreciate their colleagues' challenges and contributions. Consequently, misunderstandings are reduced, leading to clearer communication and more effective collaboration.

Open, Consistent, and Respectful Communication: Embracing an open culture establishes a solid foundation for respectful and consistent team interactions. This focus on transparency promotes the free flow of ideas and ideas, fostering a stronger sense of belonging and teamwork. When team members feel safe sharing their thoughts without fear of judgment, it creates a collaborative atmosphere that enhances relationships and overall team performance.

Constructive Conflict Management: Taking a proactive stance toward workplace conflicts creates an environment where team members see disagreements as opportunities for growth rather than just conflicts. This outlook promotes constructive conversations, enabling individuals to share different viewpoints and work together more effectively to resolve issues, thereby improving both personal and team relationships.

Active Trust-Building: Trust doesn't occur spontaneously; it must be consciously built and cultivated over time. This includes participating in team-building exercises that enhance relationships and camaraderie among members. Moreover, being transparent in decision-making helps everyone feel involved and appreciated, promoting open communication. Finally, mutual respect among team members is crucial, creating a safe space for sharing ideas and concerns and strengthening trust within the team.

In project management, prioritizing relational alignment not only enhances team cohesion but also enables teams to operate more efficiently. Such alignment allows for quicker adaptation to change, fostering resilience in the face of challenges and ensuring a more successful overall project outcome.

Sustainable Success: Results Without Sacrificing People

Sustainable success addresses the question: how can we achieve lasting results beyond the lifespan of a project? While many projects may initially deliver short-term wins, this often comes at the expense of long-term sustainability. When teams focus solely on meeting deadlines and quick results, they risk creating an environment prone to burnout, disengagement, and low morale. Over time, these issues can significantly harm performance and increase turnover, ultimately eroding the very success they were intended to achieve.

Symbiotic Leadership adopts a unique approach by emphasizing results that both focus on outcomes and foster team cohesion during the process. This leadership style recognizes that long-term success depends on several vital factors. Primarily, ensuring the team's well-being is essential. A supportive and healthy work environment where members feel appreciated can boost engagement and productivity.

Furthermore, maintaining trust and nurturing strong interpersonal relationships within the team is vital, as it promotes open communication and collaboration, resulting in improved outcomes. Lastly, developing systems that support future efforts ensures the team is not just responding to current challenges but is also prepared for ongoing and upcoming projects, establishing a sustainable path to success.

To effectively adopt Symbiotic Leadership, leaders should balance performance expectations with the team's capacity. This involves setting realistic goals that do not compromise team members' well-being or the quality of work. Leaders must also avoid short-term decisions that could cause longer-term issues later on. Instead, adopting a forward-looking view focused on team growth and development is essential. By investing in their talents and offering opportunities for professional growth, leaders can cultivate a team that is capable, motivated, and prepared for future challenges.

In practice, sustainable success manifests as several positive outcomes after a project ends. An effectively led team stays engaged and motivated, with members enthusiastic about new challenges instead of feeling exhausted. Relationships within the team become more robust and collaborative, developed through mutual respect and shared wins. Additionally, the organization as a whole becomes better equipped for future projects by leveraging lessons learned and its team's improved skills, fostering a cycle of ongoing success.

Symbiotic Leadership: Brings It All Together

Symbiotic Leadership offers a transformative leadership model that builds on existing traditional theories instead of replacing them. It highlights the significance of blending essential factors like motivation, trust, ethics, and purpose into a single cohesive system. This integrated approach reinforces the idea of shared success, where individual and team achievements are interconnected. Unlike traditional leadership methods that tend to emphasize individual motivation and rigid performance metrics, Symbiotic Leadership focuses on creating an environment that supports both personal development and collective excellence.

Instead of focusing solely on questions about individual needs or controlling results, like "How do we motivate individuals?" or "How do we control performance?", Symbiotic Leadership urges leaders to ask more comprehensive questions. A crucial question becomes: "How can we foster an environment where both people and performance thrive together?" This important change in perspective deepens understanding of team and organizational dynamics. It shifts leaders from just managing tasks to emphasizing cohesion and synergy among team members.

By adopting this approach, leaders can build effective, resilient teams sharing goals. Emphasizing collaboration fosters an environment where individuals feel valued and aligned with the mission. Consequently, team members are more likely to participate actively, boosting performance and innovation. Symbiotic Leadership emphasizes not just goals but also building relationships and a healthy work culture.

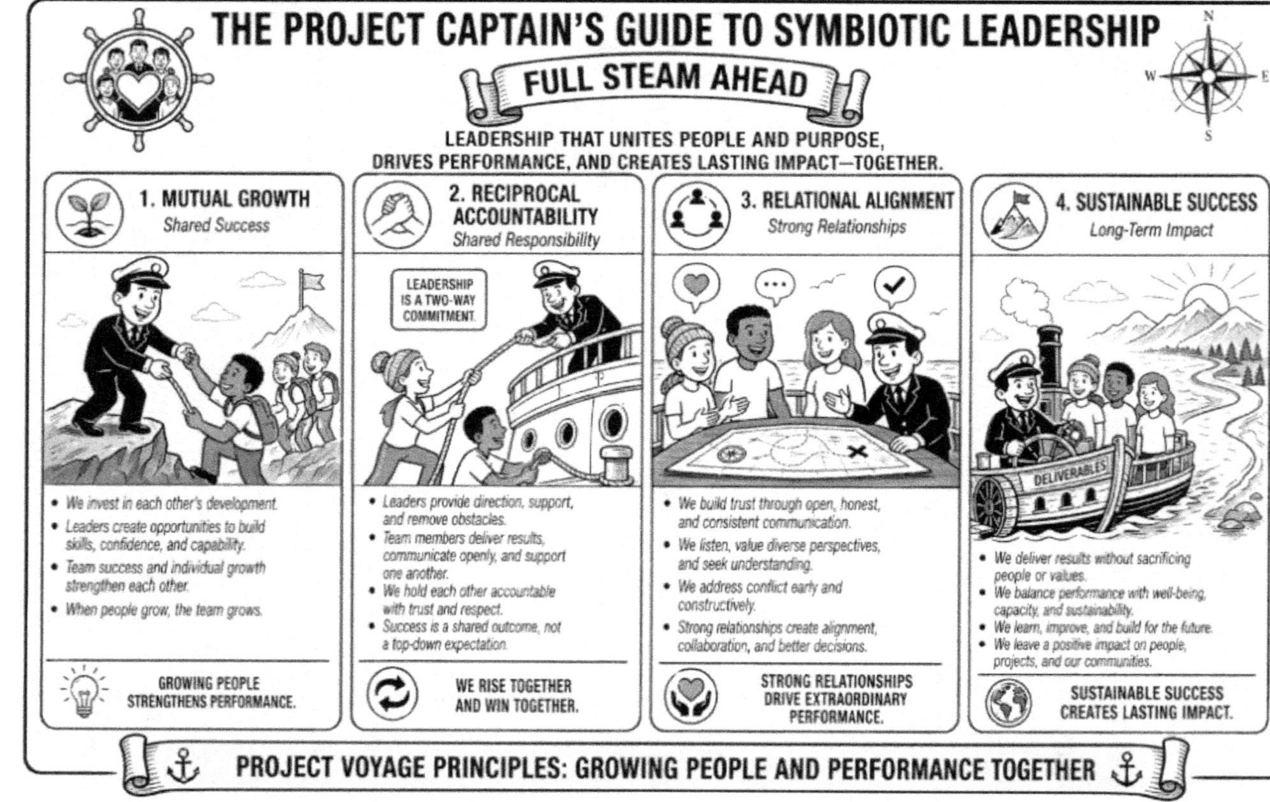
THE PROJECT CAPTAIN'S GUIDE TO SYMBIOTIC LEADERSHIP
FULL STEAM AHEAD
LEADERSHIP THAT UNITES PEOPLE AND PURPOSE, DRIVES PERFORMANCE, AND CREATES LASTING IMPACT—TOGETHER.

1. MUTUAL GROWTH
Shared Success
We invest in each other's development.
Leaders create opportunities to build skills, confidence, and capability.
Team success and individual growth strengthen each other.
When people grow, the team grows.
GROWING PEOPLE STRENGTHENS PERFORMANCE.

2. RECIPROCAL ACCOUNTABILITY
Shared Responsibility
LEADERSHIP IS A TWO-WAY COMMITMENT.
Leaders provide direction, support, and remove obstacles.
Team members deliver results, communicate openly, and support one another.
We hold each other accountable with trust and respect.
Success is a shared outcome, not a top-down expectation.
WE RISE TOGETHER AND WIN TOGETHER.

3. RELATIONAL ALIGNMENT
Strong Relationships
We build trust through open, honest, and consistent communication.
We listen, value diverse perspectives, and seek understanding.
We address conflict early and constructively.
Strong relationships create alignment, collaboration, and better decisions.
STRONG RELATIONSHIPS DRIVE EXTRAORDINARY PERFORMANCE.

4. SUSTAINABLE SUCCESS
Long-Term Impact
DELIVERABLES
We deliver results without sacrificing people or values.
We balance performance with well-being, capacity, and sustainability.
We learn, improve, and build for the future.
We leave a positive impact on people, projects, and our communities.
SUSTAINABLE SUCCESS CREATES LASTING IMPACT.

PROJECT VOYAGE PRINCIPLES: GROWING PEOPLE AND PERFORMANCE TOGETHER

Real-World Example: Leading a Project Team

Imagine you are leading a project team tasked with building a house. The team includes contractors, suppliers, inspectors, and stakeholders, each with distinct motivations and responsibilities. Some team members prioritize completing tasks efficiently (achievement), while others value collaboration and relationships (affiliation). Some individuals may seek leadership roles or influence decisions (power).

Relying on a single leadership style can make team alignment difficult. For instance, a highly controlled environment might stifle creativity, whereas granting excessive autonomy could cause misalignment. By applying Symbiotic Leadership, you focus on building strong relationships, aligning individual motivations with project goals, and fostering mutual accountability.

You communicate clearly, support team members, and ensure that success is shared across the team. As a result, the team not only completes the project successfully but also does so in a way that strengthens relationships and improves long-term performance.

Connecting to Your Project 2

As you continue developing Project 2, begin reflecting on your personal leadership experiences. Consider: 1. How you've influenced others at work. 2. The impact of different leadership styles on results. 3. The role of relationships in success or failure. This chapter marks a transition from managing tasks to leading people.

Reflection Questions

Reflect on a leader you've worked with or observed. What kind of leadership style did they display? How did it influence the team's performance and morale? Are there parts of their leadership approach you'd want to adopt or modify?

Closing Thought

Leadership isn't about titles; it's about the impact you make. Although theories can offer guidance, true leadership comes from relationships, decisions, and results. As you progress, keep in mind that success is a collective achievement. The most effective leaders foster environments where everyone has the opportunity to grow, contribute, and succeed together.

⚓ Key Takeaways

- ✓ Project management requires both technical skills and leadership ability
- ✓ Leaders inspire, guide, and support their teams beyond task completion
- ✓ Emotional intelligence improves communication, trust, and decision-making
- ✓ Different situations require different leadership styles

✓ Strong leadership fosters collaboration, accountability, and team success

End-of-Chapter Questions

1. What is the difference between managing a project and leading a team?
2. Why is leadership important in project management?
3. What are key qualities of an effective leader?
4. What is emotional intelligence, and why does it matter in leadership?
5. How do leadership styles impact team performance?
6. What role does trust play in leadership?
7. How can a leader motivate and support a team?
8. What challenges can arise from poor leadership?
9. How does leadership influence project outcomes?
10. Why is adaptability important for effective leadership?

📖 *Captain's Log: Discussion Board*

Recall a time when you were under the guidance of a strong or ineffective leader. Consider which behaviors were noticeable and how they affected your motivation and performance. Think about the kind of leader you aspire to be and how your actions could influence your team's success and overall well-being.

Chapter 13 – Agile Archipelago
(Agile / Scrum)

🎯 *Learning Objectives*

By the end of this chapter, you should be able to:

- ✓ Understand the principles of Agile project management
- ✓ Identify key characteristics of Agile methodologies
- ✓ Explain the difference between Agile and traditional (predictive) approaches
- ✓ Recognize common Agile frameworks such as Scrum
- ✓ Understand how Agile emphasizes collaboration, adaptability, and continuous improvement

CHAPTER 13

Agile Archipelago

⚓ *Entering Agile Archipelago*

As the Deliverables departs from Leadership Lookout, the river splits into several channels. Instead of a single clear route, the crew encounters numerous islands spread across the water, each demanding careful navigation, adjustments, and heightened awareness.

Captain Brian studies the waters carefully. "We've entered Agile Archipelago," he says.

The crew looks around, confused. "There's no single path forward," one crew member says.

The captain nods. "That's because the path changes as we move."

Another crew member points toward a shifting current. "So how do we know where to go?"

The captain smiles. "We don't follow a fixed route here. We adjust as we go, based on what we learn."

The crew exchanges uncertain looks.

"This is where flexibility replaces rigidity," the captain continues. "And where progress matters more than perfection."

What Is Agile?

Agile answers a core question: how can we consistently deliver value in constantly changing environments? This project management approach has become widely popular because of its flexibility and emphasis on ongoing improvement. Agile is especially useful in today's rapid environment, where being able to pivot can determine success or failure.

A core principle of Agile is its emphasis on flexibility. Unlike traditional project management approaches that follow strict plans, Agile promotes adaptability, enabling teams to rapidly adjust priorities based on new insights or evolving conditions. This flexibility helps keep the project relevant and aligned with stakeholder requirements.

Another key element of Agile is its iterative approach. Instead of trying to deliver a full product in one go, Agile teams focus on short, time-boxed development cycles called sprints. Each sprint delivers a small piece of functionality that can be assessed and improved. This iterative method offers regular review opportunities and facilitates the early identification of potential problems.

Continuous feedback is an essential element of the Agile methodology. Agile teams actively seek input from stakeholders and users throughout the development process.

This feedback loop enables teams to make informed adjustments based on real user experiences, ultimately resulting in a product that better meets users' needs. By prioritizing this collaboration, teams can ensure that each iteration improves on the last.

Collaboration is crucial for Agile's success. Cross-functional teams work closely, dismantling silos and promoting open communication. This culture of collaboration boosts creativity and innovation while also building stronger team relationships, as members feel more committed and involved in the project's results.

In summary, Agile fosters a flexible and collaborative approach to managing projects. By utilizing short cycles and prioritizing ongoing feedback, Agile teams are able to deliver incremental value that can be refined according to stakeholder input. This method enables teams not only to adapt to change but to capitalize on it, ultimately achieving better results in a continually changing environment.

The Agile Manifesto

The Agile philosophy is based on four core values that inform decision-making and how projects are carried out. The first value highlights the significance of people and their interactions rather than relying solely on processes and tools. Although processes and tools are important for organizing work, Agile places greater importance on the human aspects that foster innovation and problem-solving. It understands that strong communication and teamwork lead to better outcomes, as collaborators can adapt to and respond to challenges more effectively than strict procedures allow.

The second value emphasizes prioritizing working solutions rather than exhaustive documentation. Traditional project management often sees extensive documentation as burdensome and time-consuming. Agile methodology advocates for creating functional solutions that provide real customer value. It stresses that a working product, even in basic form, is more important than detailed documents. This approach enables teams to iterate rapidly and improve their results using real user feedback.

Customer collaboration over contract negotiation is the third core value. Instead of focusing on contract details or rigid agreements, Agile emphasizes continuous communication and teamwork with customers throughout development. This method helps ensure the final product closely matches client needs and expectations, promoting a partnership and common goals.

Finally, Agile emphasizes responding to change over rigidly sticking to a plan. In software development and project management, circumstances frequently evolve, requiring adjustments to initial plans. Agile fosters flexibility, allowing teams to modify strategies and approaches as new information becomes available or market conditions shift. This adaptability helps teams stay resilient and responsive, resulting in more successful outcomes.

Basically, these Agile values offer a framework for making decisions effectively. They don't aim to remove processes or detailed planning but promote a balanced approach that emphasizes people, collaboration, and flexibility. This focus shift helps teams work more efficiently, allowing them to adapt to the changing needs of projects and stakeholders.

The 12 Principles Behind the Agile Manifesto

Agile is more than just a collection of values; it is rooted in twelve core principles that guide team collaboration and efficient value delivery. These principles highlight flexibility, a customer-focused approach, and ongoing improvement, promoting a comprehensive approach to project management that supports adaptive planning and quick responses to change. Following these principles helps teams boost their productivity and better meet the changing needs of stakeholders.

1. **Customer Satisfaction Through Early and Continuous Delivery:** Our highest priority is to satisfy the customer through early and continuous delivery of valuable work.

2. **Welcome Changing Requirements:** Change is accepted, even late in the process, because it can improve the final outcome.

3. **Deliver Frequently:** Deliver working results frequently, with a preference for shorter timescales.

4. **Business and Team Collaboration:** Stakeholders and team members must work together daily throughout the project.

5. **Build Projects Around Motivated Individuals:** Give people the environment and support they need and trust them to get the job done.

6. **Face-to-Face Communication:** The most effective way to communicate is through direct interaction.

7. **Working Results Are the Primary Measure of Progress:** Progress is measured by what has been completed, not by how much has been planned.

8. **Sustainable Pace:** Teams should be able to maintain a consistent pace indefinitely without burnout.

9. **Technical Excellence and Good Design:** Continuous attention to quality improves agility and long-term success.

10. **Simplicity:** Maximize the amount of work not done, focus only on what adds value.

11. **Self-Organizing Teams** The best solutions come from teams that organize and manage their own work.

12. **Regular Reflection and Improvement:** Teams should regularly reflect on how to become more effective and adjust accordingly.

Captain's Note

Consider these principles as your guiding compass in Agile. They don't specify a precise route, but they assist you in making the right choices when the direction shifts.

Agile in Practice: Iterative Delivery

Agile project management is a methodology that focuses on flexibility and customer satisfaction by using iterative cycles. Projects are broken into short timeframes called iterations or sprints. This organized yet flexible method aims to support incremental progress, allowing teams to evaluate success continuously rather than waiting until the project is fully complete.

In an Agile project, each iteration targets a small, manageable set of tasks. By dividing the workload into smaller parts, teams can concentrate on delivering specific features or improvements within a short period. This focused approach makes large projects seem more achievable and streamlines efforts, enabling team members to use their time and resources more efficiently.

Each iteration aims to create a usable result. Unlike traditional project management, which often produces a final deliverable after a lengthy timeline, Agile promotes delivering functional products in smaller, incremental steps. This approach allows stakeholders to review both the progress and the product's current functionality at the end of each iteration. As a result, Agile helps ensure the final product better meets the client's needs and expectations, leading to higher satisfaction.

A key element of Agile iterations is the focus on feedback and adaptation. After each cycle, teams gather input from stakeholders and users to guide planning for upcoming sprints. This ongoing feedback process enables teams to pivot or modify their strategies promptly, resolving issues early. By fostering open communication and adjusting to evolving needs,

Agile teams can effectively minimize risks and improve their responsiveness to unexpected challenges.

This iterative approach ultimately reduces the risk of project failures and promotes ongoing improvement. Teams can learn from each iteration, continually refining their processes and results. By adopting the Agile methodology, organizations develop a more flexible, responsive, and effective project management style that emphasizes delivering value while also encouraging learning and growth.

Scrum Basics: A Practical Framework

One of the most commonly used frameworks in the Agile methodology is **Scrum**, which provides a structured approach to managing complex projects. Scrum emphasizes collaboration, flexibility, and iterative progress, allowing teams to adapt to changing requirements and deliver high-quality results efficiently.

Scrum Roles

Product Owner: The Product Owner is responsible for defining project priorities and ensuring that stakeholders' needs and expectations are accurately represented and addressed. This role involves gathering requirements, making critical decisions about functionality, and maintaining a clear vision for the product's direction.

Scrum Master: The Scrum Master plays a key role in facilitating the Scrum process and guiding the team through Agile practices. This individual helps remove obstacles that may hinder the team's progress and fosters a collaborative environment, ensuring everyone adheres to Scrum principles.

Development Team: The Development Team includes skilled professionals who carry out the tasks necessary for the project. They are responsible for designing, coding, testing, and delivering features efficiently, working together closely to meet project goals and deadlines.

Scrum Events

Sprint Planning: In this phase, the team defines and prioritizes tasks for the next sprint. They discuss, estimate, and select tasks based on their significance and the team's capacity, ensuring everyone understands the goals and expected deliverables.

Daily Standup: This brief daily meeting brings the team together to discuss progress toward sprint goals. Members share their recent achievements, upcoming tasks, and any challenges to promote transparency and enable quick issue resolution.

Sprint Review: At the end of the sprint, the team presents the completed work to stakeholders and project owners. This showcase provides an opportunity for feedback, helping ensure the product meets expectations and allowing suggestions for future enhancements.

Retrospective: Following the sprint review, the team evaluates the sprint process as a whole. They discuss successes and challenges and determine concrete actions to improve future sprints. This ongoing focus on improvement helps refine workflows and strengthen team cohesion.

Scrum Artifacts

Product Backlog: This list comprehensively details all work items, features, enhancements, and fixes slated for future development. It serves as the primary repository for everything the team might address, with items prioritized based on their value and alignment with project objectives.

Sprint Backlog: A selected portion of the Product Backlog comprising work items to be completed in the current iteration or sprint. This list highlights the team's commitments for delivery within the set timeframe, ensuring clarity on immediate priorities.

Increment: An "increment" signifies the tangible, finished results of work completed within a sprint. It includes all finalized product features, improvements, and fixes that are potentially ready for release, reflecting the project's overall progress.

Agile vs. Traditional Approaches

When it comes to project management methodologies, a fundamental question arises: when should we commit to detailed planning, and when is it better to remain adaptable? This question is best answered by comparing two prominent approaches: the traditional (Waterfall) method and the Agile method. Each has its strengths and weaknesses, and the project context often determines which is most suitable.

Traditional (Waterfall) Approach

The traditional approach, known as the Waterfall method, focuses on detailed planning at the start of a project. In this approach, all phases are well-defined and carried out in a strict sequence. Each phase must be finished before the next begins, which helps ensure predictability and a clear schedule for project completion.

Stakeholders benefit from a well-defined environment with clearly outlined roles and responsibilities. This clarity makes traditional project management a good fit for projects with clear, stable requirements. For instance, construction projects frequently adopt this approach due to their fixed specifications and linear processes.

Agile Approach

In contrast, the Agile approach differs significantly from traditional methods by focusing on adaptive planning and iterative cycles. Instead of fixed phases, Agile promotes flexibility and quick responses to change, allowing teams to modify their priorities and strategies based on ongoing feedback and changing requirements. This approach is especially beneficial in dynamic settings where client needs or market conditions can change unexpectedly.

Agile encourages collaboration and regular evaluation of progress within teams. This method supports quick iterations, boosts innovation, and helps ensure the final product meets user expectations. It is especially useful in software development and other dynamic industries where flexibility and quick response are essential.

Ultimately, neither the Waterfall method nor Agile is always better. The decision depends largely on the project context, the type of deliverables, and the likelihood that requirements will change. Knowing each project's unique features and needs helps teams choose the most suitable methodology to achieve their goals and ensure success.

Where Agile Goes Wrong

Agile methodologies have become increasingly popular recently due to their many benefits, including greater flexibility, faster delivery, and improved team collaboration. Despite these advantages, Agile is frequently misunderstood and poorly implemented in many organizations. This confusion can cause common problems that reduce the method's effectiveness.

A common problem is focusing too much on processes rather than the people executing the work. While structured processes are important for guiding teams, overemphasizing them can create a rigid atmosphere that hampers creativity and collaboration. Remember, the main aim of Agile is to improve team interactions and promote open communication. When teams put processes ahead of people, they risk creating a setting in which innovation is blocked, and team members feel undervalued.

Moreover, many organizations fall into the trap of scheduling excessive meetings that provide little value. While frequent check-ins and discussions are key to Agile practices, too many can lead to frustration and disengagement among team members. It's crucial to find a balance: meetings should have a specific purpose, and everyone should feel their time was worthwhile. The goal should be productive collaboration, not just sticking to a meeting schedule.

A major challenge is the absence of clear direction and accountability in Agile teams. For Agile to work well, each team member needs a clear understanding of their roles and responsibilities. A shared vision helps coordinate efforts and ensures all members aim for common goals. Without clarity, accountability suffers, leading to confusion about who owns tasks and deliverables. Setting clear objectives and reviewing them regularly is crucial to staying focused and making steady progress.

Furthermore, Agile is often seen as merely a set of practices rather than a comprehensive mindset. This shallow view can weaken the changes Agile aims to promote. To genuinely adopt Agile, teams need to internalize its core principles and develop habits of flexible planning and ongoing improvement. It involves creating a culture that promotes experimentation and learning, rather than merely checking off items to appear compliant with Agile practices.

Ultimately, these challenges prompt a critical question: What happens when flexibility becomes chaos? Agile is designed to be a responsive methodology, but without proper discipline, communication, and strong leadership, that responsiveness can devolve into disorder. To harness Agile's full potential, organizations must commit to creating a structured yet flexible environment that enables teams to thrive. This commitment requires ongoing training and support and emphasizes aligning Agile values with daily practices to ensure successful implementation.

Agile in the Real World

In real-world settings, Agile rarely appears in its pure form. Teams usually operate in hybrid models that blend aspects of different methodologies to suit their project needs better. This mix of approaches enables a more flexible and comprehensive strategy, which is crucial in today's complex project environments.

Structured planning is essential for these hybrid models. While Agile approaches prioritize adaptability, having a baseline plan provides teams with clear direction and objectives. It includes defining project scope, timelines, and key milestones, helping teams stay focused and responsible. Incorporating this into their workflow creates a framework that combines strategic foresight with the flexibility to adapt as necessary.

Another key aspect is iterative execution. This method enables teams to split projects into smaller, manageable segments and complete work in short cycles. Each cycle offers a chance to evaluate progress, collect feedback, and implement adjustments. This fosters ongoing improvement and allows teams to quickly adapt to changing requirements or unforeseen challenges that may occur throughout the project.

Lastly, ongoing monitoring is crucial to hybrid models. Continuous evaluation of project performance ensures that teams remain aligned with their objectives and identify potential roadblocks early. This approach combines the structured approach of traditional project management with the flexibility of Agile, enabling timely interventions and course corrections when necessary.

Ultimately, effective project management requires both stability and flexibility. By adopting hybrid models that combine planned structures, iterative processes, and continuous monitoring, teams can better handle project complexities while staying adaptable. This balanced strategy allows them to capitalize on the advantages of different methodologies, increasing their likelihood of success.

Leadership in Agile Environments

Agile leadership tackles a core question: how can leaders steer their teams without micromanaging every detail? This new mindset is vital in today's rapid and ever-evolving workplaces, where flexibility and adaptability are essential.

Effective Agile leaders empower their teams by granting autonomy to make decisions and take ownership of their tasks. This isn't just about stepping back; it involves building confidence in team members, enabling them to use their unique skills and insights. In doing so, leaders foster an environment that encourages creativity and innovation, resulting in improved problem-solving and stronger solutions.

Collaboration is a fundamental aspect of Agile leadership. Agile leaders encourage open communication and teamwork, working to eliminate silos that can hinder progress. By promoting a collaborative culture, they encourage team members to openly share knowledge, ideas, and feedback. This spirit of cooperation helps teams align their goals and work more effectively toward a shared objective, ultimately boosting productivity and morale.

A key responsibility of Agile leaders is to eliminate obstacles that could hinder their teams' progress. This includes recognizing potential barriers such as organizational procedures, resource limitations, or external issues, and taking proactive steps to resolve them. Removing these obstacles helps create a clearer path for the team, enabling them to concentrate on producing high-quality results without avoidable disruptions.

Finally, trust is key in Agile leadership. It encourages teams to take risks and innovate without fearing failure. Agile leaders aim to create a safe space where team members feel appreciated and respected, strengthening relationships and teamwork. This trust improves team interaction and cultivates a culture of responsibility, with individuals owning their roles.

Essentially, Agile leadership signifies a significant shift from traditional management practices that primarily involve directing work. Instead, it emphasizes empowering teams to succeed. This approach allows leaders to offer the right tools, support, and environment, leading to greater engagement, better outcomes, and a more adaptable organization.

Agile Lifecycle

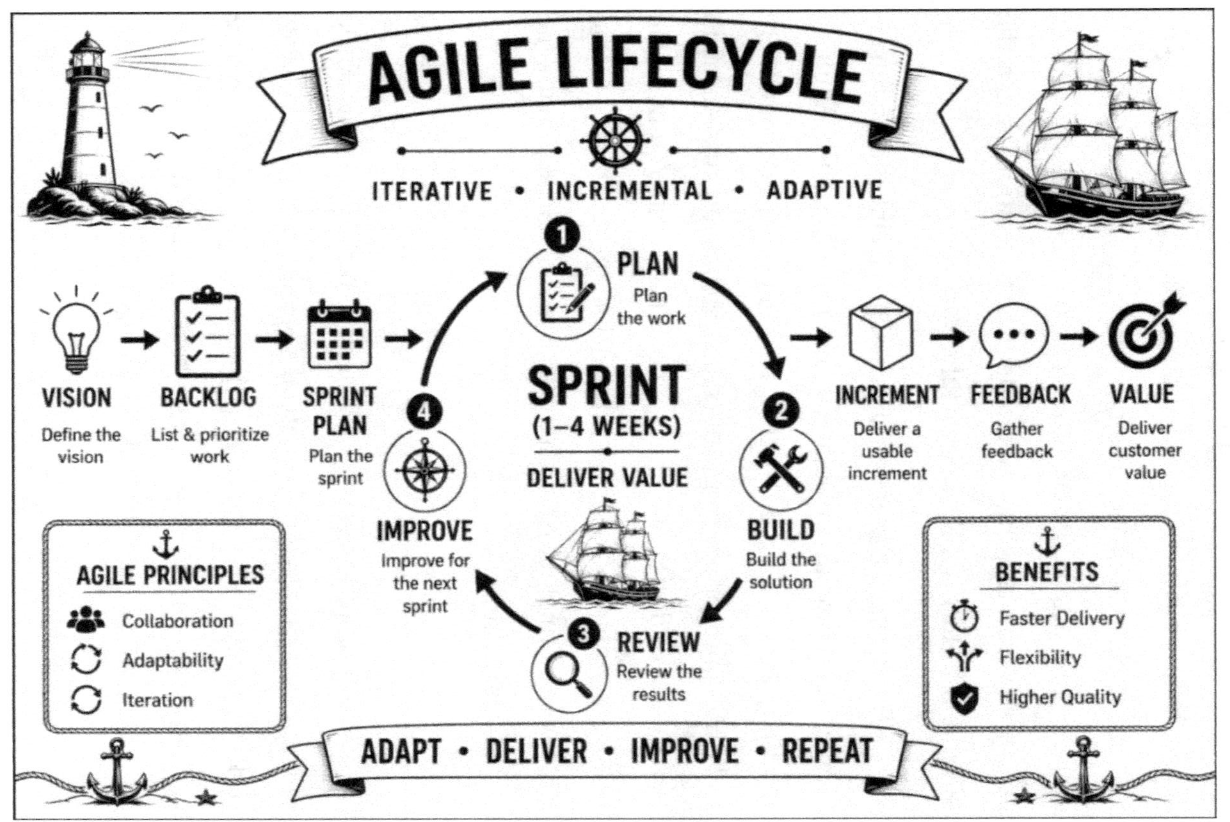

Real-World Example: Agile in Home Design

Imagine you are working with a client to design a custom home, but instead of finalizing every detail upfront, you take an iterative approach. You begin with a basic design and gather the client's feedback. Based on that feedback, you adjust the layout, features, and materials. Each iteration brings the design closer to what the client truly wants.

However, challenges arise. The client's preferences change, new ideas are introduced, and priorities shift. Without structure, these changes can lead to delays and confusion. By applying Agile principles, you manage this process through short cycles of design, feedback, and adjustment. You maintain flexibility while ensuring progress. This approach allows you to deliver a final design that aligns more closely with the client's expectations.

Connecting to Your Project 2

As you progress with Project 2, reflect on how Agile principles might already be part of your experience. Consider work that required ongoing adjustments, scenarios where feedback influenced results, and tasks completed in stages rather than all at once. These experiences can be adapted into Agile project approaches.

Reflection Questions

Reflect on a time when requirements or expectations shifted during a task or project. How did you respond to the change? Did flexibility improve or complicate the outcome? How might an iterative approach have helped?

Closing Thought

Agile isn't about discarding structure but about tailoring it to suit real-world conditions. In constantly changing environments, the capacity to adapt, learn, and evolve is more important than sticking rigidly to a plan. As you steer through the Agile Archipelago, keep in mind that success isn't measured by strictly following a set route but by making ongoing progress toward your goal.

⚓ *Key Takeaways*

✓ Agile focuses on flexibility, iteration, and customer value

✓ Work is completed in small increments called iterations or sprints

✓ Agile prioritizes individuals and interactions over processes and tools

✓ Continuous feedback improves product quality and alignment

✓ Agile supports adaptability in changing environments

End-of-Chapter Questions

1. What is Agile project management?

2. What are the core principles of Agile?

3. How does Agile differ from traditional project management approaches?

4. What is an iteration or sprint?

5. What is Scrum, and how is it used in Agile?

6. What roles are typically involved in an Agile team?

7. Why is customer feedback important in Agile?

8. How does Agile support flexibility and adaptability?

9. What challenges can arise when implementing Agile?

10. How does Agile improve collaboration and team performance?

Captain's Log: Discussion Board

Recall a time when plans unexpectedly shifted during a task or project. How did you or your team respond, and what effect did these changes have on the final outcome? Consider how adopting an Agile approach, centered on flexibility, feedback, and iteration, might have enhanced the process and the results.

Chapter 14 – Accountability

Anchorage (Value & Ownership)

⊕ *Learning Objectives*

By the end of this chapter, you should be able to:

- ✓ Understand the importance of accountability in project management
- ✓ Identify how ownership influences project outcomes
- ✓ Explain the relationship between accountability and value delivery
- ✓ Recognize how transparency supports accountability
- ✓ Understand how accountability aligns teams toward shared goals

CHAPTER 14

Accountability Anchorage

⚓ *Entering Accountability Anchorage*

As *the Deliverables* moves beyond Agile Archipelago, the waters begin to calm. The ship approaches a well-structured harbor where vessels are docked with precision. Crews are organized, responsibilities are clear, and every action appears intentional.

Captain Brian slows the ship. "We've arrived at Accountability Anchorage," he says.

The crew looks around. "It feels… steady here," one crew member says.

The captain nods. "Because this is where ownership takes hold."

Another crew member asks, "Isn't that what we've been doing all along?"

The captain pauses.

"Not exactly. We've been completing tasks. This is where we take responsibility for outcomes."

The crew reflects on the difference.

"At this stage," the captain continues, "it's not about what was assigned, it's about what gets delivered."

Responsibility vs. Accountability

The difference between responsibility and accountability tackles a key question in project management: who is supposed to do the work, and who is ultimately responsible for the results? This distinction is essential for understanding team roles and ensuring that everyone is working towards the same project objectives.

Responsibility usually refers to the specific tasks and duties assigned to an individual. It includes the actions a person is expected to complete within a project. In team settings, multiple members often share responsibility for different tasks, forming a collective effort that drives the project forward. However, this shared responsibility can sometimes cause confusion about who is responsible for each part of the project, making it important to clearly define these roles.

Accountability, on the other hand, means owning the final outcome. Although several people might contribute to different parts of a project, responsibility is usually assigned to one person or role. This person is responsible for making sure the final results align with the project's goals and standards. Assigning a single accountable individual helps keep a clear chain of command, which is essential for decision-making and resolving issues when challenges occur.

Understanding the distinction between responsibility and accountability is key to maintaining clarity within a project team and avoiding confusion regarding outcomes. When team members know their specific responsibilities and understand who is accountable for the overall result, it creates a more organized environment with clear expectations, reducing the chance of miscommunication. This clarity improves team dynamics and helps drive the project toward successful completion more efficiently.

What Is Accountability?

Accountability is about ensuring that the work done leads to the intended results. It emphasizes ownership and responsibility in every task, urging individuals to consider not only completing their assignments but also the impact of their efforts on a project's or organization's overall objectives. This deeper understanding of accountability goes beyond merely checking off tasks on a list; it is about creating meaningful outcomes that contribute to long-term success.

Taking responsibility for results is a key element of accountability. It involves recognizing one's part in a project's success or failure and being ready to accept the consequences. When team members acknowledge their role in either achieving goals or facing setbacks, they foster a culture of trust and teamwork. Embracing this ownership encourages individuals to give their best and pursue excellence.

Additionally, accountability means following through on commitments. It means not just stating intentions but also taking the necessary steps to meet those promises. This dedication to following through builds trust among team members and stakeholders, fostering a culture where everyone can depend on each other to deliver as agreed. Such reliability is essential for developing strong working relationships and ensuring smooth project advancement.

Taking ownership of results is crucial for maintaining accountability. It involves preparing to clarify actions and outcomes and to handle questions or concerns. This openness encourages constructive feedback and discussions that can boost future performance and decision-making. When people take ownership, they foster a culture of transparency focused on learning and continuous improvement.

Lastly, addressing issues proactively is a hallmark of accountability. Rather than waiting for problems to escalate, they take the initiative to identify and resolve challenges early. This proactive approach helps mitigate risks and keeps the focus on delivering value rather than merely completing tasks. Ultimately, accountability is a commitment to excellence, shifting the emphasis from merely finishing work to making a meaningful impact that aligns with the shared goals of the team and organization.

Accountability and Ownership

Ownership fundamentally involves cultivating an accountable mindset. It prompts individuals to ask themselves: Do I see this outcome as my responsibility? This sense of ownership strengthens the bond between a person and their work, inspiring them to take personal responsibility for the results.

When people take ownership, they act proactively rather than waiting for instructions. This proactive mindset enables them to lead confidently, often fostering innovative ideas and a lively work setting. By spotting and resolving issues early, they stop problems from getting worse, helping projects stay on schedule.

Furthermore, clear communication is a key sign of ownership. Individuals with this mindset openly share their progress and any challenges they face. This openness encourages a collaborative environment, allowing team members to come together, brainstorm solutions, and support each other in overcoming difficulties.

In the end, those who take ownership stay committed to the project's success. They view their contributions as essential, turning assigned tasks into personal duties. This dedication improves work quality and fosters pride and a sense of achievement within the team. Promoting ownership helps organizations unleash a strong drive for success and innovation.

Accountability and Value Creation

Understanding the true purpose of any project requires recognizing the link between ownership and value delivery. Projects are seldom finished just for the sake of finishing; instead, they aim to provide tangible value to stakeholders. This shift in perspective can greatly affect the results of any initiative.

When a project team has a high level of accountability, their results often mirror this dedication. Deliverables are carefully prepared to meet or surpass expectations, ensuring all goals are achieved. Team members take responsibility for their tasks, resulting in quick problem-solving whenever issues occur. This proactive attitude creates an environment where stakeholders receive valuable outcomes aligned with their needs and objectives. In the end, a strong sense of accountability leads to efficient project execution, with everyone working together toward a shared goal.

On the other hand, weak accountability can have harmful effects. While tasks may be completed, they often lack the intended value. Issues tend to go unresolved for long periods, reducing the project's overall success. Consequently, the final results often fail to meet expectations, leading to stakeholder dissatisfaction. Without accountability, the project's core purpose is compromised, leading to wasted effort that doesn't deliver real value. This contrast underscores the vital importance of accountability in ensuring that every effort results in meaningful outcomes.

The Trickle-Down / Trickle-Up Value Loop

This model explores a key question: How does value move through different project stages, and who is responsible at each point? Since the work in a project is deeply interconnected, no task, decision, or deliverable exists in isolation.

Each component is linked in a chain that connects the entire project team to the final customer. Understanding this chain is crucial for clarifying accountability within the project. By grasping how each part contributes to the overall goal, teams can more clearly identify roles and responsibilities, ensuring everyone stays focused on delivering value effectively.

Trickle-Down Value Requirements

Value originates from the highest level within an organization: the customer. It is the customer who articulates their needs and expectations, setting off a cascade of communication that flows through the entire company. This process unfolds in several key steps:

The **customer** effectively communicates a specific need or expectation they consider essential to their satisfaction or the success of a product or service. After the need is expressed, the **company** assumes responsibility for interpreting and formally approving the request. This initial step is vital because it determines how the organization views the customer's requirement and the level of importance it assigns to it.

Once approved, the **project manager** takes over to convert the customer's needs into concrete tasks. This process includes breaking down the requirement into manageable parts that the team can easily understand. Finally, skilled team members carry out the assigned tasks, turning the project into reality through the specified actions.

Throughout this hierarchical flow, the requirements undergo refinement at each step to ensure a coherent, aligned response to the original expectation. However, this cascading effect also introduces **potential risks** that can compromise the original value intended by the customer:

Misinterpretation: Misunderstanding the customer's key needs can result in a product or service that fails to meet expectations.

Loss of Detail: As information moves through the organization, important details can be lost, leading to an incomplete understanding of the requirement.

Assumptions: Each party might base their assumptions on personal perspectives or experiences, resulting in outcomes that diverge from the customer's vision.

Clear communication and mutual understanding across all levels of an organization are vital. Without these, the customer's perceived value can become distorted as it moves through different departments and teams. This disconnection often leads to misunderstandings and misinterpretations, which can negatively affect the customer's experience and satisfaction. Maintaining clarity and consistency in messaging is crucial to preserving the integrity of the value provided to the customer throughout their journey.

Trickle-Up Value Delivery

Once the project starts, the flow of value actually moves in the opposite direction. It begins with **team members** who carefully complete and deliver their assigned tasks. This stage is important because it sets the foundation for future steps. Each completed task contributes to the overall project goal, indicating progress and efficiency.

After completing the work, the **project manager** is crucial in validating and merging the team's components. This process guarantees that all parts meet the project's goals and standards. The project manager thoroughly reviews the deliverables, makes any necessary adjustments, and combines the team's various contributions into a single, cohesive result. This integration is essential to maintain quality and consistency in the final deliverables.

Once the project manager has successfully validated the work, **the company** takes the next major step by consolidating all components and preparing for delivery. This phase involves final checks and processes to ensure that everything meets the requirements and expectations established at the outset. The company's efforts culminate in a structured delivery of the final product or service, showcasing the outcomes of the team's and management's hard work.

Finally, the deliverable is handed over to **the customer**, who receives the final product or service. This moment marks the culmination of the process, reflecting the value generated by the team's initial efforts, the project manager's supervision, and the company's dedication to quality. The true value becomes clear at this stage when the customer evaluates and experiences the results of all the collaborative efforts.

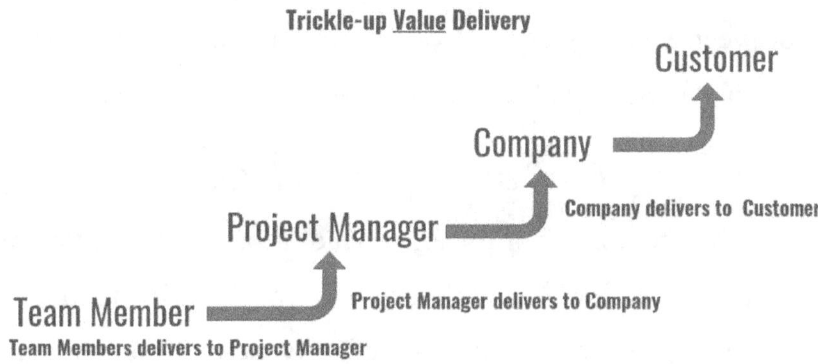

In every structured process, deliverables advance through multiple levels, with each stage playing a vital role in the final result. This creates a transparent chain of accountability that becomes more apparent when evaluating performance at each point. The significance of each level is paramount: a failure at any stage can ripple through the entire structure, affecting all subsequent deliverables. This connection highlights the necessity for careful attention and proactive actions at every step.

Conversely, when one level shows improvement, the benefits extend beyond its immediate outputs, positively influencing the entire outcome. A minor improvement at one stage can generate significant momentum that flows through different levels and boosts overall performance. This underscores the importance of ongoing improvement, as each progress not only improves its own level but also enhances the entire system. Therefore, understanding the connections between levels is crucial for creating an environment where accountability is valued and teamwork leads to success.

The Value Feedback Loop

The process is not linear; instead, it operates in a flexible loop. At every stage of delivery, a thorough verification takes place to ensure quality and effectiveness. This approach enables continuous improvement and adaptation throughout the procedure.

✓ Team members meticulously review their own work before progressing to the next phase, ensuring that each component meets the required standards.

✓ Project managers conduct a comprehensive validation of the outputs, scrutinizing them before they are escalated to the next level.

✓ The organization as a whole engages in a thoughtful review of outcomes before delivery, ensuring alignment with objectives and stakeholder expectations

✓ Following delivery, the customer provides valuable feedback based on their experience, offering insights that help to refine the process further.

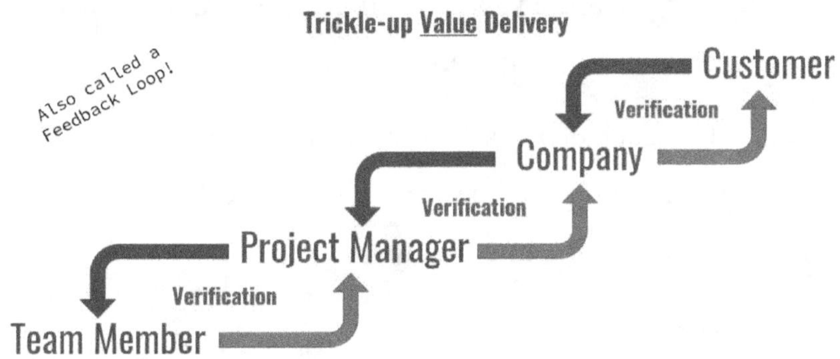

You can also look at each Trickle up delivery as a verification loop as well.

In these verifications, bugs, changes, and risks can arise.

This creates a continuous **feedback loop** that fosters improvement and agility, in which:

✓ Errors are detected early in the process, allowing for timely resolution.

✓ Adjustments are implemented swiftly, minimizing disruptions and enhancing overall efficiency.

✓ Quality consistently improves over time as lessons learned are incorporated into future cycles.

However, at these crucial verification points, new challenges may emerge, including:

✓ Bugs that require immediate attention to ensure system reliability.

✓ Changes in requirements that demand flexibility and adaptability from the team.

✓ Newly identified risks that necessitate proactive management and mitigation strategies.

These challenges are not setbacks; instead, they are essential parts of the process that offer chances for development and improvement.

What This Means for Accountability

The Trickle-Down/Trickle-Up model highlights a key principle essential to any successful organization. All team members are responsible to the customer, even if they don't interact with them directly. This viewpoint counters the belief that only frontline workers, such as sales or customer service teams, are customer-facing. It acknowledges that everyone involved, whether behind the scenes or in various departments, significantly influences the customer experience.

Understanding this interconnectedness is crucial because each team member's work directly influences the final product. For example, the careful coding by a developer, the intuitive design by a designer, or the thorough testing by a quality assurance specialist all shape what the customer ultimately experiences. Every task, even those that seem minor, fits into a bigger picture that affects customer satisfaction. This comprehensive perspective underscores that everyone's efforts are important and that the impact of their work can be far-reaching.

This shared accountability leads to the central notion that "team members are their own project managers." Adopting this mindset helps individuals see how their roles contribute to the organization's overall goals. It motivates them to understand how their daily tasks and choices support the primary aim of satisfying customer needs and expectations. Taking responsibility for quality and completeness transforms from merely a requirement into a personal dedication to excellence.

Moreover, employees must consider the downstream impact of their actions. This means thinking critically about how their decisions will affect others within the organization and the customer's final experience. By doing so, team members can anticipate challenges, identify potential improvements, and foster a culture of continuous improvement. Ultimately, this proactive approach not only benefits the customer but also promotes a collaborative environment where everyone is motivated to contribute to the team's collective success.

Barriers to Accountability

Accountability in teams or organizations is often weakened by common obstacles that prevent personal ownership and responsibility. A major issue is unclear roles and expectations. When team members are unsure about their duties or goals, it's harder for them to take initiative. This lack of clarity causes confusion and disengagement, making it difficult for individuals to feel responsible for their work.

Another major obstacle is poor communication. Effective communication is essential to fostering an environment where accountability can thrive. Insufficient communication among team members can result in the loss or misinterpretation of important information, leading to misalignment on goals and responsibilities. This breakdown in communication can create a culture in which accountability is further weakened, as individuals may feel unsupported or unsure of how their actions affect the larger team atmosphere.

Furthermore, insufficient leadership support can greatly hinder accountability. When leaders do not actively encourage a culture of ownership or fail to supply essential resources, team members might be reluctant to take responsibility. Strong leadership is vital to creating an environment where individuals feel confident to own their tasks and decisions without fearing negative consequences.

Fear of failure or blame often acts as a widespread obstacle to responsibility. People may hesitate to take ownership of tasks, worried about negative feedback or making errors. This anxiety can hinder innovation and progress, as individuals focus on self-protection rather than pursuing bold actions that could benefit themselves and the team.

Finally, relying too heavily on processes rather than encouraging a sense of ownership can be harmful. When organizations prioritize strict protocol compliance, it can reduce individual initiative and creativity. Team members might become mere followers of procedures rather than active contributors who take pride in their work, ultimately limiting accountability.

Overcoming these obstacles involves setting clear expectations, fostering trust within teams, and providing supportive leadership. When organizations cultivate an environment where everyone understands their roles and feels confident to take ownership without fear of failure, they can develop a stronger accountability culture. This not only boosts performance but also promotes a more engaged and motivated workforce.

Building a Culture of Accountability

This initiative seeks to address a fundamental question: How can we create an environment that promotes and maintains ownership? The solution is to develop a culture of accountability in which people feel confident taking responsibility for their actions and contributions. This starts with leadership, which plays a crucial role in shaping the behavior and culture of any team or organization.

Leaders play a crucial role in building accountability by clearly defining each team member's roles and expectations. When individuals understand their responsibilities and the standards by which their work will be measured, they are more likely to take ownership of their tasks. Clarity reduces confusion and strengthens direction and purpose. Ultimately, this transparency fosters an environment where everyone knows what is expected of them and what they can strive to achieve.

Open communication is a key component in progressing accountability within a team. Leaders should cultivate an environment where team members feel safe to share their thoughts, ideas, and concerns. This transparency enhances relationships and facilitates more effective problem-solving. When issues occur, a well-communicating team can work together more efficiently to address and overcome challenges. This environment promotes shared responsibility, with individuals recognizing that their contributions are vital to the team's collective success.

Additionally, leaders should proactively help their team members overcome challenges as they arise. Offering guidance and resources empowers teams to confront issues directly. This support underscores that ownership extends beyond personal effort to include seeking help and collaborating when necessary. It sends a crucial message: difficulties are a normal part of progress and can be managed collectively.

Recognizing and reinforcing ownership behaviors are vital for maintaining a culture of accountability. Celebrating individuals who show accountability boosts morale and sets a positive example for others. When team members see their peers acknowledged for initiative and responsibility, they are more inclined to emulate these behaviors. This recognition fosters a strong feedback loop, transforming accountability from just a requirement into an integral part of the team's culture.

In high-pressure project settings, accountability goes beyond mere duty; it becomes integral to daily interactions and expectations. Promoting a culture that values transparent communication, supportive leadership, and acknowledging individual ownership helps teams foster a thriving environment where accountability thrives. In this context, team members feel empowered to take responsibility for their roles, leading to enhanced collaboration, innovation, and overall achievement.

Real-World Example: Applying the Value Loop to Construction

Imagine you're overseeing the construction of a house. The homeowner shares their vision with the company, which the project manager then translates into detailed plans. These plans are handed off to contractors, who carry out the work.

As requirements move downward, details can be lost or misunderstood. A design choice may be interpreted differently, or a specification may not be fully communicated. As work moves upward, each layer must verify the results. Contractors complete their tasks, the project manager reviews the work, and the company ensures the final product aligns with the original vision.

If verification is bypassed at any stage, problems may go unnoticed until the homeowner receives the final product, making corrections more expensive and difficult to implement.

By maintaining accountability at every stage, the team ensures that value flows correctly from requirements to delivery.

Connecting to Your Project 2

As you continue working on Project 2, begin identifying how accountability appears in your experience.

Consider:

- Tasks you were responsible for

- Outcomes you were accountable for

- Situations where you took ownership beyond your assigned role

This will help you translate your experience into meaningful contributions to projects.

Reflection Questions

Think about a time when a project or task depended on multiple people. Was accountability clearly defined? Did individuals take ownership of outcomes? How did accountability, or lack of it, impact the result?

Closing Thought

Accountability transforms effort into tangible results. Responsibility outlines what should be done, but accountability guarantees it is executed properly, resulting in significant outcomes. As you move forward, remember that success is not measured by the number of tasks completed but by the value delivered.

⚓ Key Takeaways

✓ Accountability ensures that responsibilities are owned and outcomes are delivered

✓ Clear ownership improves performance and reduces confusion

✓ Accountability is directly tied to delivering value, not just completing tasks

✓ Strong accountability and transparency promote trust and strengthen team alignment

End-of-Chapter Questions

1. What is accountability in project management?

2. Why is accountability important for project success?

3. How does ownership impact team performance?

4. What is the relationship between accountability and value delivery?

5. How does transparency support accountability?

6. What challenges can arise from a lack of accountability?

7. How can a project manager encourage accountability within a team?

8. What role does communication play in accountability?

9. How does accountability improve project outcomes?

10. Why is it important for teams to align around shared goals?

📖 *Captain's Log: Discussion Board*

Recall a time when accountability was either strong or absent in a team or project. Consider how that affected performance, trust, and outcomes. Reflect on how increased ownership, transparency, and alignment might have improved the situation and achieved better results.

Chapter 15 – Closing Dock
(Project Closure)

⌖ Learning Objectives

By the end of this chapter, you should be able to:

- ✓ Understand the purpose of the project closure phase
- ✓ Identify key activities required to formally close a project
- ✓ Explain the importance of stakeholder acceptance
- ✓ Recognize the value of documenting lessons learned
- ✓ Understand how proper closure supports future project success

CHAPTER 15

Closing Dock

⚓ *Arriving at the Closing Dock*

As the Deliverables approaches the final stretch of the river, the crew starts to notice a change. The waters have calmed, the path is clear, and a sturdy dock comes into view ahead.

Captain Brian slows the ship. "We've arrived at the Closing Dock," he says.

The crew looks relieved. "So… we're done?" one crew member asks.

The captain smiles. "Not yet."

The crew exchanges confused looks. "We've completed the work," another says.

The captain nods. "Yes, but completing the work and closing the project are not the same thing."

The ship gently docks.

"This is where we finalize everything," the captain continues. "Where we confirm what was delivered… and make sure nothing is left unfinished."

What Is Project Closure?

Project closure addresses a key question: how do we formally conclude the project and verify its success? This stage marks the official end of the project, encompassing key activities that confirm the work is completed. It is an important step to ensure all stakeholders are aligned and have a clear understanding of the project's outcomes.

The project closure process is thorough, involving the completion of all activities and ensuring that all deliverables meet the set objectives. Every aspect of the project must be carefully reviewed to confirm its completion. Tasks and deliverables identified at the project's start should be evaluated to verify proper completion. This process isn't merely about ticking off items; it aims to confirm that the quality and standards expected have been met.

A key part of closing a project is obtaining **formal approval** from stakeholders. This process involves interacting with project sponsors, team members, and other relevant parties to confirm their acceptance of the finished work. Gaining consensus helps establish transparency and trust, encouraging open feedback and discussion. Through stakeholder collaboration, project managers can resolve any lingering issues and confirm the project's final outputs.

Additionally, documenting the project's results is vital in this phase. This record should include overall performance, **lessons learned**, and any deviations from the initial plan. Capturing this information helps teams promote continuous improvement and offers valuable insights for future projects. Well-maintained records of outcomes serve as useful references for understanding successes, challenges, and strategies to improve execution in upcoming efforts.

Finally, closing contracts and completing administrative tasks are vital to wrapping up a project. This step involves ensuring that all financial obligations are settled, contracts are fulfilled or terminated appropriately, and any necessary reports are filed. Such administrative diligence is essential to avoid any lingering responsibilities that could lead to confusion or complications down the line.

In summary, project closure is an essential step that clarifies the project's conclusion. By methodically confirming completion, securing stakeholder approval, recording results, and managing administrative tasks, project managers can ensure a successful ending, laying a strong foundation for future projects to capitalize on the achieved success.

Finalizing Deliverables

At the heart of this crucial step lies a fundamental question: Did we deliver what we promised? This question not only gauges the project's success but also reflects our commitment to our stakeholders. To answer this effectively, it is imperative that all project deliverables be thoroughly reviewed. This needs a structured method to ensure that each component is completed and meets quality and functionality standards.

Every deliverable must go through a thorough review process. This is crucial because it enables the team to evaluate the work critically and verify that it meets the project's objectives and specifications. Review sessions should be collaborative, encouraging feedback and allowing for the identification and correction of any issues before the final submission. Additionally, verifying the deliverables is vital to ensure they conform to the original requirements outlined at the start of the project.

Once the deliverables are finished, reviewed, and verified, obtaining formal acceptance from stakeholders is the final step. This stage is crucial because without formal approval, the project might still be considered open by stakeholders, even if it appears complete. Acceptance confirms that stakeholders are satisfied with the results and acknowledges the team's efforts. It signals a shift from project execution to closure, indicating that the project not only delivered as promised but also met the expectations and needs of those it serves.

Administrative Closure

Projects are complex undertakings that encompass more than just deliverables. Each project involves critical components such as documentation, contracts, and records that are vital to tracking progress and ensuring accountability. **Administrative closure** is a crucial phase in the project lifecycle, serving as a final checkpoint that answers the question: Have we formally wrapped up all project-related work? This process is essential to ensure that every aspect of the project has been completed and acknowledged.

A key part of administrative closure is **final documentation**, which involves gathering all relevant materials, such as reports, meeting minutes, and correspondence, that contributed to the project's progress. This complete record safeguards the organization and acts as a reference for future projects, offering insights into successful strategies and areas for improvement.

Contract closure is another critical step in this process. It involves reviewing all agreements with vendors, stakeholders, and team members to ensure obligations are fulfilled. This not only confirms that all parties have met their commitments but also helps build smoother relationships for future collaborations. Proper closure also ensures that any outstanding payments are settled and that warranties or guarantees are addressed.

Financial reconciliation is a crucial step in closing a project. It requires carefully examining the project budget, comparing actual expenses to the original estimates, and analyzing any differences. This detailed financial review allows the organization to assess the project's overall financial performance and pinpoint where cost savings were possible or what lessons can be applied to future projects.

Finally, **resource release** is an essential part of the administrative closure process. This step formally releases team members, tools, and facilities that were allocated to the project. Properly acknowledging and managing this release is necessary to ensure resources are used effectively for future projects.

To officially close a project, organizations must complete and archive the final documentation, close contracts, reconcile finances, and release resources. This detailed process demonstrates a dedication to effective project management. It also assists teams in building a strong foundation for future success.

Lessons Learned

Lessons learned are essential for any organization involved in project management. They address the key question: what should we take with us into future projects? Collecting these insights is fundamental to building a learning organization, allowing teams to reflect on their experiences and refine their methods to achieve better results.

Projects frequently provide valuable insights that can shape future endeavors. They identify successful strategies, creating a model for others to follow in upcoming projects. At the same time, they point out failures, helping teams recognize pitfalls to avoid. These reflections also promote a thoughtful review of processes, inspiring teams to consider potential improvements. This thorough understanding of both strengths and weaknesses cultivates a culture dedicated to ongoing enhancement.

Collecting lessons learned is vital for organizations seeking to improve their effectiveness and efficiency. Documenting key insights helps them prevent repeating errors from past projects. This proactive strategy conserves time and resources while improving future performance. Additionally, creating a knowledge repository strengthens organizational wisdom, enabling teams to make better-informed decisions based on past experiences. In the long run, this practice promotes a culture of continuous learning and growth, ultimately benefiting the entire organization.

Knowledge Transfer

Knowledge transfer addresses a key question: how can we ensure that insights and lessons from a project are preserved over time? It highlights the need to capture and share valuable information so that the effort, time, and resources invested continue to provide lasting benefits.

Knowledge transfer goes beyond a simple process; it entails actively sharing different elements crucial to a project's success. For example, project insights, key observations, and reflections on what went well and what did not are essential for guiding future initiatives. Sharing these insights enables teams to learn from past errors and replicate successful strategies.

Thorough documentation is vital for effective knowledge transfer. This includes reports, manuals, meeting notes, and research findings. Like lessons learned, this documentation acts as a reference for team members and stakeholders, allowing them to review and learn from past activities. It helps preserve crucial details, facilitating onboarding for new team members and refreshing the memories of experienced ones.

Sharing **best practices** is crucial for successful knowledge transfer. These practices represent the collective wisdom gained through experience and experimentation. Promoting the exchange of successful methods among team members fosters a culture of continuous improvement. This collaborative approach benefits individual projects and enhances the organization's overall performance.

In summary, knowledge transfer is a strategic effort aimed at preserving the value generated in a project and prolonging its influence beyond completion. By focusing on sharing project insights, maintaining thorough documentation, and sharing best practices, organizations can create a resilient framework that ensures the longevity and value of their knowledge.

Common Closure Mistakes

Projects often encounter significant challenges close to completion, primarily due to preventable errors that can threaten their success. A frequent mistake is skipping the formal acceptance process, which requires stakeholders to explicitly approve that the deliverables meet the agreed requirements. Not securing this approval can cause misunderstandings or dissatisfaction later, affecting the project's value and overall success.

A common issue is incomplete documentation. Detailed records are essential for tracking the project's progress, decisions, and results. When documentation is lacking, it can hinder future reference, learning, and replication. Without proper records, team members and stakeholders may be unsure about what happened, leading to confusion and possible disagreements.

Capturing lessons learned is essential for effective project closure. Often, teams hurriedly skip this step, forgoing a valuable chance to reflect on successes and areas for improvement. Failing to document these insights can lead organizations to repeat mistakes, hindering their growth and development.

Additionally, rushing to start the next project can introduce significant risks. Teams might accidentally miss unresolved issues or unfinished tasks because they want to complete the current project quickly. This haste can leave loose ends that threaten the project's long-term success and stakeholder happiness, causing frustration and harming credibility.

Essentially, these mistakes stem from overlooking the need for closure. Treating closure as just a formality undermines its importance. Proper project closure is vital because it guarantees the project ends as effectively as it started. It requires a thorough review of all components to facilitate a seamless transition and prepare for future projects. Focusing on closure allows teams to reinforce their successes and cultivate an ongoing improvement mindset, ultimately resulting in more successful projects over time.

Real-World Example: Closing a House Construction Project

Imagine you have completed building a house. The structure is built, the systems are functioning, and the homeowner is ready to move in. However, the project is not complete until:

✓ The homeowner formally accepts the work

✓ Final inspections are completed

✓ Documentation is provided

✓ Any remaining issues are addressed

If these steps are skipped, problems may arise later, leading to disputes, additional costs, or dissatisfaction. Completing a structured closure process ensures the project ends successfully and leaves a positive impression.

Connecting to Your Project 2

As you approach the end of your learning journey, begin reflecting on how projects conclude in jobs you have held. Consider:

- How work is finalized in your experience

- Whether formal closure processes were followed

- What lessons were captured, or lost

Understanding closure helps you recognize the full lifecycle of a project.

Reflection Questions

Think about a project or task you completed. Was there a clear conclusion, or did it simply end? Were lessons learned documented or discussed? How could the closure process have been improved?

Closing Thought

Project closure goes beyond simply finishing. It is the final phase in delivering value. It guarantees that all work is finished, accepted, and clearly understood. Without a proper closure, even successful projects might leave unresolved issues. Keep in mind that how a project concludes is just as crucial as its initiation.

⚓ Key Takeaways

✓ Closure formally confirms that the project is complete and accepted

✓ Stakeholder approval is critical to officially closing a project

✓ All deliverables must be reviewed, finalized, and documented

✓ Lessons learned capture valuable insights for future improvement

✓ Proper closure ensures a clean transition and prevents lingering issues

End-of-Chapter Questions

1. What is the purpose of the project closure phase?
2. What activities are involved in closing a project?
3. Why is stakeholder acceptance important in project closure?
4. What are deliverables, and how are they finalized during closure?
5. What is a lessons learned document?
6. Why is it important to document lessons learned?
7. What can happen if a project is not properly closed?
8. How does closure support future projects?
9. What is the role of documentation during closure?
10. How does effective closure contribute to overall project success?

📓 *Captain's Log: Discussion Board*

Recall a time when you finished a task or project but skipped reflecting on what worked well and what didn't. How did this affect your ability to improve later? Consider how formally closing a project—by reviewing, documenting, and noting lessons learned—can enhance your future performance and results.

Chapter 16 – The Finish Line

🎯 *Learning Objectives*

By the end of this chapter, you will be able to:

- ✓ Recognize how all phases of project management connect as a complete journey
- ✓ Understand the importance of continuous learning and growth
- ✓ Identify how project management skills apply beyond formal projects
- ✓ Reflect on the development of leadership and decision-making abilities
- ✓ Understand how to carry project management principles into future work

CHAPTER 16

The Finish Line

⚓ *Reaching the Finish Line*

As the *Deliverables* leaves Closing Dock, the crew looks ahead and sees something they have been working toward from the very beginning, a flag standing tall at the end of the river.

Captain Brian slows the ship. "The Finish Line," he says.

The crew gathers at the ship's bow. "We made it," one crew member says.

The captain nods. "Yes, but this is not the end."

The crew appears surprised. "We've completed the journey," another says.

The captain smiles, "We've completed this journey."

He gestures beyond the flag. "However, there are more rivers ahead."

The crew looks ahead again, focusing not only on their achievements but also on what is still to come.

"This wasn't just about reaching the finish line," the captain continues. "It was about learning how to navigate the journey over and over again."

Looking Back: The Full Journey

This reflection answers a fundamental question: What should you now understand as a project manager? From defining scope at the beginning to closing a project at the end, each phase builds upon the previous one, creating a complete picture of how successful projects are led.

The initiation phase sets the direction for everything that follows. At this stage, you are responsible for clearly communicating the project's vision, purpose, and objectives. When done well, this phase establishes alignment and ensures that everyone involved understands not only what needs to be done but also why it matters. This clarity becomes the foundation that supports every decision moving forward.

During the planning phase, structure becomes your greatest asset. You will develop timelines, allocate resources, and define key milestones that guide execution. A well-built plan does more than organize work; it creates confidence within the team. It ensures alignment, reduces uncertainty, and provides a roadmap that keeps everyone moving in the same direction.

As the project moves into execution, plans begin to take shape in the real world. This is where leadership becomes visible. You will see collaboration, problem-solving, and adaptability come into play as the team works toward delivering results. Expect energy, challenges, and moments that require quick decision-making. This phase is where preparation meets reality.

Monitoring and controlling ensure that progress remains aligned with expectations. Regular check-ins, performance tracking, and adjustments are not optional; they are essential. As a project manager, you should expect to continuously evaluate progress, identify risks, and make informed decisions to keep the project on track. This discipline creates stability and prevents small issues from becoming major problems.

Leadership remains the constant throughout every phase. You are not just managing tasks; you are guiding people. Effective leadership hinges on clarity, strong communication, and staying focused during challenges. Teams perform at their best when they feel supported, empowered, and aligned with a shared purpose.

Accountability reinforces ownership across the team. Each individual must understand their responsibilities and how their work contributes to the overall outcome. When accountability is clear, performance improves, trust increases, and teams operate with greater confidence and consistency.

Finally, the closure phase brings everything together. This is where deliverables are finalized, outcomes are reviewed, and lessons are captured. It is also a critical moment to recognize contributions and reflect on what was accomplished. Closure is not just the end of a project but the bridge to future success.

Each phase, from initiation to closure, contributes to a deeper understanding of what it takes to lead a successful project. These are more than mere steps in a process; they are experiences you'll face, challenges you'll handle, and skills you'll keep improving throughout your career.

Project Management Beyond the Classroom

Project management goes beyond formal projects. It influences everyday work, shaping decision-making and responsibility management. In all areas of a professional career, situations arise where applying project management principles becomes essential. These principles act as a guiding framework, helping navigate the complex landscape of daily tasks and challenges.

A common challenge in project management is handling evolving requirements. In evolving workplaces, priorities often shift, and new needs can appear unexpectedly. This fluid situation can cause confusion, requiring us to adapt quickly to stay aligned with organizational goals. Good project management helps us develop the skills to manage these changes, allowing us to evaluate their impact on our tasks and modify our strategies as needed.

Unclear expectations can create major obstacles. When a project's or task's goals are not well-defined, it can cause misunderstandings and misalignment within the team. This uncertainty can reduce productivity and slow progress. Implementing project management practices helps establish clear communication, define specific objectives, and promote teamwork, ensuring everyone knows their roles and responsibilities.

Resource limitations often pose challenges, including time, budget, and personnel constraints, which can hinder efficient task completion. Effective project management helps overcome these constraints through strategic planning and prioritization. This approach ensures resources are used wisely and that focus remains on activities with the greatest impact.

Stakeholder challenges frequently occur, such as managing differing opinions, conflicting interests, or varying engagement levels. Stakeholders are vital to any project, and their support can greatly affect success. Using project management methods, stakeholders can be identified early, their needs and concerns can be understood, and they can be effectively involved throughout the project.

While often linked to formal projects, project management principles are highly valuable for everyday work challenges. Using these principles helps us adapt to changing needs and clarify expectations. This enhances resource allocation and promotes stakeholder engagement, leading to more successful professional results.

Continuous Improvement

Each project offers a unique opportunity to learn from its results, regardless of whether they meet expectations. Successes and setbacks both provide valuable lessons that guide your future efforts. By carefully examining what worked and what did not, you can improve processes, test new strategies, and refine existing approaches to increase efficiency and effectiveness. This ongoing process strengthens your skills and deepens your understanding, supporting continuous growth as a project leader.

Growth is built on three key principles: reflection, adaptation, and application. Reflection gives you the opportunity to review your full experience, strengthening self-awareness and decision-making. Adaptation requires using those reflections to make adjustments, improving your approach to achieve goals more effectively. Lastly, applying these insights to future projects is essential. Learning from the past is valuable, but real growth and innovation happen when you put those lessons into action.

Ultimately, the goal is not perfection but consistent progress. Embracing this mindset allows you to recognize small victories along the way and to understand that improvement is a journey rather than a destination. By focusing on your development over time, you create a foundation of continuous learning and resilience, where each experience contributes to your growth as a project leader.

Your Role Moving Forward

As you start your duties as a project manager, an important question arises: What type of project manager will you become? This role requires a balanced combination of skills and qualities, and you have now created a solid foundation to build on. With this foundation, you can plan efficiently, making sure your projects are well-structured and organized. This includes defining clear goals, timelines, and resources, which helps you see the future course clearly and identify possible obstacles.

Furthermore, it's essential to have a clear sense of purpose in your role. A project manager goes beyond simply facilitating; you're a leader who encourages and motivates your team. By communicating a clear vision and fostering a collaborative atmosphere, you can motivate team members to do their best. Your ability to adapt to change will also be crucial for success. Since projects can be unpredictable, being flexible allows you to overcome obstacles and adjust your plans, demonstrating resilience in the face of challenges.

However, knowledge alone isn't enough for effective project management. Real success depends on your ability to apply what you've learned in practical situations. Every project offers unique lessons that help you improve your strategies and decision-making skills.

Furthermore, continuous development is necessary in the rapidly changing field of project management. Actively pursuing growth through professional courses, mentorship, or self-reflection can help you stay up to date on industry trends. This commitment to improvement will ultimately enhance your effectiveness as a leader.

Additionally, keep in mind that a project manager's path is one of continuous growth and learning. By combining knowledge with practical experience, you position yourself to deliver successful project outcomes. Just as important is the ability to build and sustain a positive, productive team environment, which forms the foundation for long-term success. As you move forward, every project becomes part of a larger journey, one in which you are not simply navigating the river but confidently taking the helm.

Real-World Example: Your First Project After This Course

Imagine becoming a project manager for the first time after finishing your course. The excitement is strong, but so is the uncertainty as you confront tight deadlines and high expectations from your team and stakeholders. Instead of letting yourself feel overwhelmed initially, or allowing doubt to cloud your judgment, you pause, take a deep breath, and reconnect with the basics of project management.

First, you define the project's scope. This step clarifies the objectives, deliverables, and boundaries of the work ahead. You gather input from all relevant stakeholders to ensure everyone's expectations align. As you do so, you take note of key milestones and outcomes, creating a clear vision of where you want to go. With a solid understanding of what your project entails, you transition into the planning phase.

Next, you create a detailed project plan. This includes mapping out a timeline with deadlines, assigning tasks to team members, and determining resource requirements. As you build your plan, you monitor potential risks and develop strategies to mitigate them. You know that a well-constructed plan is crucial for guiding your team and keeping everyone on track.

Communication becomes your lifeline as you engage with stakeholders throughout the project. You establish regular check-ins and updates, fostering an environment where feedback flows freely. By encouraging open dialogue, you ensure that everyone feels invested and informed, reducing the likelihood of misunderstandings or surprises.

As the project unfolds, you diligently monitor its progress. You review completed tasks against your timeline and check in with team members to celebrate accomplishments and identify roadblocks. When challenges occur, they naturally encourage you to change your approach. This might involve reallocating resources, tightening deadlines, or reevaluating the project scope. You stay flexible and responsive to the ever-changing demands of project management.

Throughout this journey, you have gone beyond just applying knowledge; you have built a valuable skill set. Your confidence has increased as you tackled complex decisions and led with clarity. With each project, your judgment improves, and your leadership becomes stronger. You now see that project management is more than theory; it's a practical skill that turns uncertainty into successful results. The journey does not end here; you are prepared to take the helm, navigate what lies ahead, and lead confidently.

Connecting to Your Project 2

As you finish your final project, take a moment to reflect on your experience. Think about what you learned, what challenged you, and how you applied project management principles. This reflection is a crucial step in moving from learning to practice.

Reflection Questions

Which concept from this course influenced your understanding of project management the most? How has your view on teamwork and leadership evolved? What skills are you eager to further improve? How do you plan to implement these ideas in your future work?

⚓ *Key Takeaways*

✓ The project lifecycle is a continuous journey, not a one-time event

✓ Skills developed through project management apply across careers and industries

✓ Growth comes from experience, reflection, and application

✓ Leadership and decision-making improve with each project

✓ The end of one project marks the beginning of the next opportunity

End-of-Chapter Questions

1. What is the overall project lifecycle, and how do the phases connect?

2. Why is project management considered a continuous journey?

3. How do project management skills apply outside of formal projects?

4. Why is continuous learning important in project management?

5. How do leadership skills develop over time through project experience?

6. What role does reflection play in personal and professional growth?

7. How can past project experiences improve future outcomes?

8. Why is adaptability important for long-term success?

9. How does project management contribute to effective decision-making?

10. Why is the end of one project considered the beginning of another opportunity?

📖 *Captain's Log: Discussion Board*

Reflect on your journey through this course and the concepts you have learned. How has your understanding of project management evolved, and what skills have you developed? Looking ahead, how will you apply these principles to future projects, challenges, or leadership opportunities?

Final Thought

The finish line isn't the end but rather a transition point. The knowledge and skills you have developed now become the tools you will carry throughout your career. As you move beyond this course, remember that project management is not about executing a perfect plan, but about navigating challenges, working with others, and delivering meaningful results. The river continues ahead, and you are ready to navigate it with confidence, clarity, and purpose.

Captain's Final Words

Captain Brian looks out over the water one last time. "You now know how to navigate," he says.

The crew stands quietly, reflecting on the journey.

"You won't always have clear waters," he continues. "You won't always have perfect plans."

He pauses.

"But you will have the ability to adapt, to lead, and to deliver."

The captain steps back from the wheel. "And now," he says, "It's your turn to take the helm."

Glossary

A

Accountability – Ownership of the final outcome of a task or project, including responsibility for results and performance.

Actual Cost (AC) – The total cost incurred for work completed on a project during a given time period.

Agile – An iterative approach to project management that emphasizes flexibility, customer collaboration, and delivering value in small increments.

Agile Manifesto – A set of guiding values and principles that promote adaptive planning, early delivery, and continuous improvement in Agile projects.

Assumptions – Factors considered to be true for planning purposes, even though they may carry some level of uncertainty.

Assumptions and Constraints – Conditions that impact the project, where assumptions are accepted as true and constraints are limitations such as time, cost, or resources.

B

Baseline – The approved version of a project plan used as a reference point to measure performance.

Business Case – A document that outlines the justification for a project, including expected benefits, costs, and overall value.

C

Change Control – The process of reviewing, approving, and managing changes to project scope, schedule, or cost.

Change Request – A formal proposal to modify any aspect of a project, including scope, schedule, cost, or resources.

Closing – The final phase of a project where all work is completed, deliverables are accepted, and lessons learned are documented.

Communication – The exchange of information between stakeholders to ensure alignment and understanding throughout the project.

Communication Plan – A document that defines how project information will be created, shared, and managed.

Constraints – Limitations or restrictions that impact a project, such as time, cost, scope, or resources.

Cost Baseline – The approved version of the project budget used to monitor and control cost performance.

Cost Management – The process of planning, estimating, budgeting, and controlling project costs.

Cost Performance Index (CPI) – A measure of cost efficiency calculated as Earned Value divided by Actual Cost.

Cost Variance (CV) – The difference between Earned Value and Actual Cost, indicating whether the project is under or over budget.

Critical Path – The sequence of dependent tasks that determines the shortest possible duration of a project.

D

Deliverables – The outputs or results produced by completing project work, which must meet defined requirements.

Deliverables Boat – A symbolic concept used in this book to represent the movement of completed work through the project lifecycle.

Dependencies – Relationships between tasks that determine the order in which activities must be performed.

E

Earned Value (EV) – The value of work actually completed, measured against the planned value.

Executing – The phase where project plans are put into action and work is performed to produce deliverables.

Execution Phase – The stage of the project lifecycle focused on completing tasks and delivering project outputs.

G

Gantt Chart – A visual timeline that displays project tasks, durations, and dependencies.

Goals – Desired outcomes or targets that the project aims to achieve.

I

Initiating – The process of defining the project's purpose, objectives, and stakeholders.

Inputs – The resources, information, or materials required to begin a process.

Integration – The coordination of all project elements to ensure they work together effectively.

Integration Management – The processes required to ensure all aspects of the project are properly aligned and coordinated.

K

Key Performance Indicator (KPI) – A measurable value used to evaluate the success of a project or specific activity.

L

Leadership – The ability to guide, influence, and support a team to achieve project objectives.

M

Matrix Organization – An organizational structure where team members report to both functional and project managers.

Milestone – A significant point or event in the project timeline used to track progress.

Monitoring – The ongoing process of tracking project performance.

Monitoring and Controlling – The process of measuring progress, identifying variances, and implementing corrective actions.

N

Network Diagram – A visual representation of project tasks and their dependencies.

O

Objectives – Specific, measurable outcomes that a project is intended to achieve.

Outputs – The results produced by completing a process.

P

Performance Measurement – The evaluation of project progress using metrics such as cost, schedule, and quality.

Planned Value (PV) – The authorized budget assigned to scheduled work.

Planning – The process of defining scope, schedule, cost, and resources for a project.

Planning Phase – The stage where detailed project plans are developed.

Process – A series of actions taken to achieve a specific result.

Process Groups – The five stages of project management: Initiating, Planning, Executing, Monitoring and Controlling, and Closing.

Process Port – A visual framework used in this book to represent Inputs, Process, and Outputs.

Procurement – The process of acquiring goods or services from external vendors.

Procurement Management – The processes involved in purchasing or acquiring project needs from outside the organization.

Project – A temporary effort undertaken to create a unique product, service, or result.

Project Charter – A document that formally authorizes a project and grants the project manager authority to proceed.

Project Experience Log – A structured record used to document project-related work experience.

Project Initiation – The process of formally starting a project.

Project Lifecycle – The series of phases a project passes through from start to completion.

Project Management – The application of knowledge, skills, tools, and techniques to meet project requirements.

Project Management Plan – A comprehensive document that outlines how a project will be executed, monitored, and controlled.

Project Manager – The individual responsible for leading the project and ensuring its success.

Project Map – A visual representation of the project journey used in this book.

Project Scope – The work required to deliver a project's objectives.

Project Schedule – A timeline that defines when project tasks will be performed.

Q

Quality – The degree to which project deliverables meet requirements and expectations.

Quality Management – The processes used to ensure project deliverables meet quality standards.

R

Requirements – The documented needs and expectations of stakeholders.

Resource Allocation – The assignment of resources to project tasks.

Resource Management – The process of planning, acquiring, and managing project resources.

Resources – The people, materials, equipment, and budget required to complete project work.

Risk – An uncertain event or condition that may impact the project.

Risk Management – The process of identifying, analyzing, and responding to risks.

Risk Register – A document used to track identified risks and their responses.

Risk Response – Actions taken to address identified risks.

S

Schedule – The planned timeline for completing project tasks.

Schedule Baseline – The approved version of the project schedule used for performance comparison.

Schedule Performance Index (SPI) – A measure of schedule efficiency calculated as Earned Value divided by Planned Value.

Schedule Variance (SV) – The difference between Earned Value and Planned Value, indicating whether the project is ahead or behind schedule.

Scope – The defined boundaries of the project, including what is included and excluded.

Scope Baseline – The approved version of the project scope used as a reference point.

Scope Creep – The uncontrolled expansion of project scope without adjustments to time or cost.

Scope Management – The process of defining and controlling project scope.

Stakeholder – An individual or group affected by or able to influence the project.

Stakeholder Engagement – The process of involving stakeholders throughout the project.

Stakeholder Register – A document that identifies stakeholders and their interests.

Symbiotic Leadership™ – A leadership framework emphasizing trust, accountability, and mutual growth.

T

Task – A specific unit of work within a project.

Timeline – A representation of the sequence and duration of project activities.

Triple Constraints – The relationship between scope, schedule, and cost, where changes in one affect the others.

V

Value – The benefit or outcome delivered by a project.

Value Delivery – The process of ensuring project outputs provide meaningful benefit to stakeholders.

Variance – The difference between planned and actual performance.

W

Work Breakdown Structure (WBS) – A hierarchical breakdown of project work into smaller, manageable components.

Index

A
Accountability, 341-365
Accountability and ownership, 347
Accountability and value creation, 348
Actual Cost (AC), 268-270
Administrative closure, 372
Agile, 316-340
Agile Manifesto, 320
Agile principles, 322
Agile in practice, 324
Agile vs. traditional approaches, 329-330
Agile leadership, 334
Alignment, 196, 252
Assumptions and constraints, 27, 60-62

B
Balancing cost and quality, 119
Baseline, 111, 196
Budget, 39-41, 111
Business case, 27-28

C
Change control, 270-272
Change requests, 250, 270-272
Closing, 60, 221, 366-380
Closing Dock, 366-380
Communication, 43-44, 136-140, 248
Communication challenges, 138
Communication plan, 43-44, 136
Conscious leadership, 299
Constraints, 60-62, 112
Contracts, 175-176
Cost baseline, 39-41, 111
Cost estimation, 39, 109
Cost management, 107-112, 223
Cost of poor quality, 116

Cost Performance Index (CPI), 268-270
Cost variance, 266-270
Critical path, 36-38, 93

D
Deliverables, 27, 47, 371
Dependencies, 35-36, 90

E
Earned Value (EV), 268-270
Earned Value formulas, 270
Ethics in leadership, 297
Execution, 60, 237-256
Execution Bay, 237-259
Execution mistakes, 253
Experience Log checklist, 215

F
Final deliverable, 47, 52-53, 371
Final submission checklist, 53
Five Process Groups, 20-21, 60, 221

G
Gantt chart, 87

I
Initiating, 20, 60, 221
Integration, 195-197, 228
Integration management, 228
Issues and changes, 250

K
Knowledge Areas, 223

L
Leadership, 241-246, 281-315
Leadership in Agile environments, 334
Leadership theories, 290-301

Lessons learned, 373
Lifecycle, 60

M
Make-or-buy decisions, 173
Managing changes, 270
Managing vendors, 180
Maslow's Hierarchy, 291
Matrix organizations, 288
McClelland's Needs Theory, 295
McGregor's Theory X and Theory Y, 293
Milestones, 87-98
Monitoring and Controlling, 60, 221, 260-280

N
Network diagram, 35-37, 92

O
Operations, projects vs., 59
Organizational structures, 286-289

P
Performance measurement, 268
Planned Value (PV), 268-270
Planning, 60, 191-203, 221
Planning Peninsula, 191-203
PMBOK® Guide, 220
PMI, 20, 216-236
PMI Island, 216-236
PMI Talent Triangle, 64
Procurement, 46-47, 169-190
Procurement mistakes, 181
Procurement planning, 46, 169
Procurement Point, 169
Procurement risks, 178
Process Groups, 20-21, 60, 221
Process Port, 67, 82, 101, 126, 145, 166, 188, 201
Project, 58
Project Charter, 28-30

Project constraints, 60-62
Project Experience Log, 208-215
Project lifecycle, 60, 221
Project Management Institute, See PMI
Project Management Plan, 25-53, 191-203
Project manager, 63, 241
Project scope, 33, 73
Project schedule, 87
Projectized organizations, 289

Q
Quality, 42, 113-119
Quality management, 113-119, 223
Quality metrics, 42
Quality standards, 113-116

R
Range of Magnitude (ROM), 39-41, 111
Requirements, 32-33, 73
Requirements document, 32-33
Resource allocation, 132-135
Resource management, 129-147
Resource River, 129-147
Resources, 132
Responsibility vs. accountability, 344
Risk, 148-168
Risk assessment, 155
Risk identification, 153
Risk management, 148-168
Risk register, 44-45, 166
Risk response strategies, 45, 157

S
Schedule, 85-103
Schedule baseline, 87-98
Schedule Performance Index (SPI), 268-270
Schedule variance, 266-270
Scheduling mistakes, 98

Scope, 70-84
Scope baseline, 33-34, 81
Scope creep, 75, 250
Scope management, 73-76, 223
Scrum, 326-328
Scrum artifacts, 328
Scrum events, 327
Scrum roles, 326
Stakeholder engagement, 31-32
Stakeholder management, 31-32
Stakeholder Matrix, 32
Stakeholder Register, 31
Stakeholders, 31
Statement of Work (SOW), 46
Symbiotic Leadership, 303-311

T
Task dependencies, 90
Theory X and Theory Y, 293
Traditional leadership theories,
290-301
Traditional project management,
329
Triple Constraint, 60-62, 112

V
Value creation, 348
Value delivery, 352-354
Value feedback loop, 354
Variance, 266-270
Vendor relationships, 180
Vendors, 46, 172-183

W
Waterfall approach, 329
Work Breakdown Structure
(WBS), 76, 92